DATE DUE

MAR 20 1995			
3/18/96			
GAYLORD			PRINTED IN U.S.A.

CHALLENGES
IN EDUCATION

ISSUES FOR THE 90s

CHALLENGES IN EDUCATION
by Victoria Sherrow

DRUGS IN AMERICA
by Michael Kronenwetter

MANAGING TOXIC WASTES
by Michael Kronenwetter

MEDICAL ETHICS:
MORAL AND LEGAL CONFLICTS
IN HEALTH CARE
by Daniel Jussim

THE POOR IN AMERICA
by Suzanne M. Coil

THE WAR ON TERRORISM
by Michael Kronenwetter

ISSUES FOR THE 90s

CHALLENGES IN EDUCATION

Victoria Sherrow

JULIAN MESSNER

To my parents

Copyright © 1991 by Victoria Sherrow
All rights reserved including the right of
reproduction in whole or in part in any form.
Published by Julian Messner, a division of
Silver Burdett Press, Inc., Simon & Schuster, Inc.
Prentice Hall Bldg., Englewood Cliffs, NJ 07632

JULIAN MESSNER and colophon are trademarks
of Simon & Schuster, Inc. Manufactured in
the United States of America.

Consultant: Penny Soule, Administrative Specialist,
Research and Development Department, Clark County
School District, Las Vegas, Nevada

Designer: Claire Counihan

10 9 8 7 6 5 4 3 2 1
Library of Congress Cataloging-in-Publication Data

Sherrow, Victoria.
Challenges in education / Victoria Sherrow.
p.   cm.—(Issues for the 90s)
Includes bibliographical references (p. 131) and index.
Summary: Examines the problems of the American education system and suggests
ways of improving it.
1. Education—United States—Aims and objectives—Juvenile literature.   2. Public
schools—United States—Curricula—Juvenile literature.   3. Educational change—
United States—Juvenile literature.   4. Educational planning—United States—
Juvenile literature.   [1. Education.   2. Schools.]
I. Title.   II. Series.
LA217.2.S56   1991
370′.973—dc20   91-7925
                                                                                      CIP
                                                                                       AC
ISBN 0-671-70556-3

CONTENTS

CHAPTER ONE

IS THE UNITED STATES

"A NATION AT RISK"?

"**S**TAY in school!" "You need a good education to get a good job." "Study hard so that you can go to college." "Get your education—it's the key to success."

These messages are probably familiar to all teenagers. You hear them from parents, teachers, books, and magazines—even from public service announcements on television. But how do you and other young people feel about your schooling? Here are some teenagers' comments:

> I'm worried. Last week I had two job interviews to train as a computer technician. At both places, the people criticized my application, saying I don't write or spell too well. I have a diploma. Maybe I didn't get top grades, but I thought high school would have prepared me for this kind of job.
>
> —K.L., age 18

Last year, I hated math! I almost failed. This year, I have a great teacher for geometry, and it makes all the difference. Our class is what people call the "slow" group, but he makes me feel like, "Hey, I can really learn this." —B.T., age 15

College is rough. Now I understand why I had to take certain classes in high school that seemed boring then. But at the time, nobody really showed me why it was important. —P.C., age 19

I dropped out last year. I was hanging out with friends, spending time in the street. It seemed like there was nothing out there for me. One of my friends and I called a hotline that said it would help people finish high school. I knew I couldn't make it, working for four dollars an hour. I'll finish school in five more months. —J.Q., age 19

Despite their different ages, backgrounds, and viewpoints, all of these young people have attended public schools in America. They are part of a complex system that received increased attention—and increased criticism—during the 1980s.

A HISTORIC MEETING

On September 27, 1989, at the University of Virginia in Charlottesville, President George Bush held a summit meeting with the nation's governors. The subject? Education in America. It was only the third time that any U.S. President has held such a meeting with governors of the states. Theodore Roosevelt led the first in 1908, to discuss conservation. Franklin D. Roosevelt led the second in 1933, to discuss the Great Depression.

The summit followed President Bush's pledge to become "the Education President." During the 1988 presidential campaign, George Bush said that inadequate education threatened the future of the country and could jeopardize America's leadership position in the twenty-first century. He called education "the nation's most powerful economic program, most important trade program and most effective antipoverty program."

During the 1980s, various studies identified shortcomings in

America's public education system. In 1983 the National Commission on Excellence in Education (NCEE), appointed by Education Secretary Terrel H. Bell, issued an alarming report called *A Nation at Risk*. It warned:

> Our once unchallenged preeminence in commerce, industry, science, and technology innovation is being overtaken by competitors throughout the world. . . . 'while we can take justifiable pride in what our schools and colleges have historically contributed to the United States and the well-being of its people, the education foundations of our society are presently being eroded by a rising tide of mediocrity that threatens our very future as a nation and as a people. . . . '

Many other critical studies followed *A Nation at Risk*, and the quality of America's schools has become a major issue. Teachers, school board members, administrators, state and federal officials, business people, parents, and students—all of these groups are examining ways to improve education.

IDENTIFYING PROBLEMS

Exactly what problems are being discussed? One major concern is that many American students are not learning what they need to know in order to perform in today's competitive workplace. They score lower on achievement tests than students from other industrialized countries, such as Japan, Germany, and Canada. Test results say that many U.S. students cannot identify the time frame of the Vietnam War or locate Nicaragua (or even Washington, D.C.) on a world map. Low scores in mathematics and science are a special concern: These are key subjects for today's high-tech world.

University educators complain that incoming freshmen are not ready for college. In a 1989 survey by the Carnegie Foundation for the Advancement of Teaching, 64 percent of the 5,450 faculty members surveyed said that students are not prepared and that they are less willing to work than students in

Kindergarteners use personal computers at a mobile computer school in Tokyo. Many Americans feel threatened by the technological prowess of the Japanese.

past years. A report by the National Assessment of Educational Progress (NAEP) stated that fewer than 5 percent of America's high school graduates would qualify for admission to European universities.

A closely related problem is that about 27 percent of all U.S. students who enter high school as freshmen drop out before graduating. They may be illiterate, or nearly so. Unable to be fully productive, they may depend on social services (welfare) for economic support, straining federal, state, and local resources.

The problem of illiteracy has serious consequences for all citizens. Approximately 75 percent of the nation's unemployed people and 60–75 percent of our country's prison inmates are illiterate. About 30 million Americans (20 percent of all adults) are functionally illiterate—unable to read, write, or solve problems well enough to perform the basic jobs in today's workplace.

American industry spends billions of dollars each year on remedial training for undereducated workers. Business owners complain that they cannot find qualified employees. A spokesman from BellSouth Corporation says, "Fewer than one in ten applicants meets our qualification standards."

LOOKING FOR CAUSES

What is to blame for these problems? People are pointing to social problems, schools, parents, and students themselves. Some experts blame a lack of "readiness"—they say many American children are not physically or mentally ready to learn when they start school.

Poverty and other social problems may hinder early development and keep people from reaching their potential. A hungry or homeless child is not fully prepared to learn, nor is a child who lacks a basic vocabulary and communication skills. Further, many "at risk" students attend schools in communities where poverty, unemployment, substance abuse, and high crime rates can continue to impede learning.

The quality of education for poor and minority children continues to be examined. Despite school desegregation efforts following the 1954 U.S. Supreme Court decision in *Brown v. Board of Education*, many black children still attend schools that are viewed as unequal. These schools may be located in low-income areas where inadequate funding limits staffing, facilities, and equipment. Housing patterns in many cities result in schools in which most or all children are poor and belong to minority groups. Citizens from various ethnic groups agree that children should interact with different kinds of people in our culturally diverse society.

What else is wrong? Some people criticize teachers and school administrators. "They don't give each child enough attention," says one dissatisfied parent. "They don't seem to care if the kids learn or not," says another. "The classes are so boring," says a high school sophomore. "Some of my teachers just talk, repeating what's in the textbook." Other people say that many students are allowed to graduate without mastering basic skills. These critics believe that schools and teachers must be held accountable for their performance.

For their part, some teachers say that they are not given the professional status, respect, or salary that they deserve. "I love teaching, but I can't support a family on my salary," says a science teacher from the Midwest. "I have a master's degree and ten years of experience, but I could earn more money as a waiter in a good restaurant." Some teachers want to help make more decisions about what is taught and how schools are run.

Many people think that today's schools are expected to do too much. Schools face many social problems, often without adequate funds, staff, and other resources. In *High School*, Ernest L. Boyer, president of the Carnegie Foundation for the Advancement of Teaching, notes that today's schools may be asked "to provide the services and transmit the values we used to expect from the community and the home and the church."

Some people also blame parents who seem to be too tired, busy, unwilling, or lacking in skills to promote a child's learning at home or to work with the school. "Some parents don't do their job," says a middle-school principal in a New Jersey suburb. "They let the kids watch too much TV and stay up late. Many don't supervise their kids' behavior or homework."

Teachers also complain about students' behavior and values. "A number of my students don't want to study. They try to get by with the least effort," says a North Carolina high school teacher. "Some do not set goals. They are interested in the next party or in how much money they can make after school. It reflects the values in our society. People want instant gratification and material things."

A teacher who taught for twenty years in New York City echoed this concern in a letter to *The New York Times* in 1989. He wrote, "What changing the size of schools, decentralizing and other gimmicks cannot overcome is that [many students] think education is a waste of time and act accordingly."

Such problems are not confined to schools in urban areas. Similar concerns are expressed elsewhere. "For about ten years, I've had children in my class who don't want to do things for themselves," says a first-grade teacher in an affluent New England suburban school. "Some kids can't tie their shoes or remember to take their papers home. They want everything to be done for them. Sometimes, it seems that both parents are so busy, no one is helping the child learn basic things."

THE 1980s: DECADE OF REFORM

Years before the Education Summit in 1989, states and school districts throughout the country were working to improve their schools. In 1989 the Center for Policy Research in Education said that during the 1980s state legislators introduced more education-related bills than ever before, increased state aid to public schools, and reviewed the reports of hundreds of state-level task forces and commissions.

Since 1983, education reforms have taken place in every state—possibly in your own community. Graduation requirements have been increased. New teaching methods and programs have been tried and evaluated. Reforms have addressed a wide variety of problems, and those that prove to be successful could become models for other schools.

Parents and other community members have become more active. Alarmed by the shortage of well-qualified employees and the expense of providing remedial education, local businesses and large corporations are working for education reform. Some offer scholarships and special incentives to students. They are also sponsoring partnership programs to reduce dropout rates and to help students see the link between education and jobs.

But more improvements are needed, as political leaders, educators, researchers, and other citizens agree. Dropout and illiteracy rates remain high. Test scores of U.S. students are considered too low. The quality of education is uneven from school to school. In a *Newsweek* interview in 1988, Ernest Boyer said, "While some children receive a first-rate education, the majority continue to attend schools that rank from fair to mediocre." In 1988 the Carnegie Foundation reported that the reform movement has not had much impact on urban schools where it is most needed. Former Education Secretary Terrel Bell concluded that "those that desperately need education . . . are the ones that we have not touched."

At the Education Summit, a fourteen-member Governors' Task Force was appointed to meet with experts from the fields of child welfare, child development, education, and industry to study education in America from preschool through high school. The Task Force recommended a number of reforms and worked with President Bush to set national education goals for the year 2000. The governors agreed that the challenges facing the nation are to prepare a "work force that will be second to none in the world" and to educate Americans to be productive citizens, capable of participating in a democratic society.

When discussing problems in education, people do not always agree on the causes and solutions. But most believe that improving education will take and effort at local, state, and federal levels. Here are some questions that need answers:

- What should America's students be taught—and how?

- How can all children be physically and mentally prepared to start school? How can schools help those at risk for school failure?

- How should schools be structured? How should decisions be made about organization, policy, curriculum, accountability?

- How can schools cope with poverty, teenage pregnancy, drug abuse, and violence?

- What resources are needed and where should they come from?

- How can the teaching profession attract and reward the most effective people? How should teachers be educated and evaluated?

- How can all Americans get the best possible education—an education that will serve them throughout their lives?

Whether you are satisfied with your education or think that your schooling could be improved, whether you are a student or are now in the work force, these issues will affect you throughout your life. The quality of education can be critical to economic success, both for the United States as a whole and for individual citizens. Some of you may become teachers, and most will become parents with children who attend public schools.

As taxpayers, you will help to decide what programs should be funded and where the money will come from. You will elect public officials who make decisions about the education system and determine the nation's goals and priorities. Your choices and decisions may well determine whether America remains a "nation at risk."

CHAPTER TWO

SETTING GOALS

FOR THE TWENTY-FIRST

CENTURY

WHAT is the purpose of public education? What standards should be met by U.S. students and schools? Says a ninth-grade student, "I want to know that when I finish school I can get some kind of job. I should be qualified for something."

"We need employees who know how to learn," according to David Kearns, former chairman of the Xerox Corporation. Other business people agree that as long as workers know how to learn, they can be trained for a specific type of job after they have been hired. Colleges also seek students who can take charge of their own learning.

"A new standard for an educated citizenry is required," said a statement issued by the National Governors Association on February 25, 1990. The governors, along with President Bush, announced these six national education goals for the year 2000:

- All children will start school ready to learn.

- The high school graduation rate will increase to at least 90 percent.

- Students will demonstrate in the fourth, eighth, and twelfth grades that they can handle such subject matter as English, mathematics, science, history, and geography; every school will make sure its students learn to use their minds so they will be ready for constructive citizenship, further learning, and productive employment.

- American students will rank first in science and math.

- Every adult American will be literate, with the knowledge and skills to compete in a global economy and exercise the rights and responsibilities of citizenship.

- Every school will be free of drugs and violence and offer a disciplined environment conducive to learning.

These national goals deal with several aspects of education: curriculum, achievement, evaluation of progress, school structure and environment and readiness for schooling. They also express a vision of what a well-educated American should be like—an effective citizen, a productive employee, and a lifelong learner.

The announcement of national goals sparked many discussions among educators and other citizens. Are the goals realistic? What human and financial resources—including federal funding—are available in order to achieve them?

Since colonial days, schools in America have grown and changed along with a changing society. The national goals for the year 2000 are part of an ongoing process to clarify goals, standards, and curricula for American education.

EARLIER VIEWS OF EDUCATION

He who ne'er learns his A,B,C,
Forever will a Blockhead be;
But he who to his Book's inclin'd,
Will soon a golden Treasure find.

This verse from a colonial schoolbook shows that from the earliest days, American schools stressed the value of learning. However, in colonial times there was no system of free or compulsory public education. Some towns organized their own schools. Others had so-called dame schools, taught by women in their homes. Usually, the goal of this brief, basic education was to enable children to read the Bible and to prepare boys to study for the ministry or for careers in medicine, law, or teaching.

In 1647, Massachusetts passed a law ordering every town with fifty or more families to provide an elementary school. Towns with more than one hundred families had to establish a secondary school as well. Usually, only wealthy families sent their sons to the secondary schools or to private academies that taught literature, Greek, Latin, elocution, and philosophy— subjects of little practical use for farmers or laborers.

Town schools were not free, but parents who had no cash could donate goods and services—firewood, repairs to the school building, or a spare room where the teacher could live.

Outside New England, schools were less common. In the Middle Atlantic and Southern colonies, people lived farther apart and were more diverse in religion and nationality. It was more difficult to agree on where to start a school and what to teach. Wealthier parents sent their sons to academies or hired tutors to teach their children at home. Thus education was regarded as a personal matter, not a government responsibility.

Families generally provided their own guidance and job training, because sons usually pursued the same trades as their fathers, while girls were expected to become mothers and housewives. They attended school for only a few years at most.

After the War of Independence, some people supported the idea of free public schools throughout the new United States. Thomas Jefferson, who would become the nation's third President, advocated "a crusade against ignorance," saying, "Above all things, I hope the education of the common people will be attended to; convinced that on their good senses we may rely with the most security for the preservation of liberty....No

The movement to provide free public education for all American children took hold in the mid-nineteenth century.

other sure foundation can be devised for the preservation of freedom, and happiness."

Jefferson and other supporters of free public education expressed a belief that is widely held today: An educated citizenry is vital for preserving our democratic way of life; voters should be able to read and to reason.

The movement to establish common schools (public schools that all children could attend) grew between 1830 and 1870, spreading from New England and New York across the West and then the South. Although schools were under local control, some states took authority over teacher credentials, attendance laws, and the curriculum, among other things.

As immigration increased during these years, so did religious diversity. Educators like Horace Mann saw the need for a curriculum that would not offend the beliefs of various groups— a core curriculum that could be taught to all children.

Mann thought that free public schools were essential in a republic. In 1837 he gave up his law practice and political career in order to become the first secretary of the Massachusetts state board of education. Throughout his life he worked vigorously for education reform, starting a journal for teachers called the *Common School Weekly* and speaking often to citizens' groups. Mann eventually gained public support for his vision of better-educated teachers, more state influence, and nonsectarian schools serving children of all religions, ethnic groups, and economic classes.

As thousands of immigrants settled in the U.S. during the late 1800s, schools were expected to "Americanize" them by teaching English and transmitting a common culture to children from diverse backgrounds. The rapid industrialization that accompanied this wave of immigration changed the school curriculum, too. Workers with specific occupational skills were needed, so schools offered courses in accounting, navigation, bookkeeping, and typing. Working families spent less time with their children, so schools became more involved in students' personal and social development. Then, as they are today, schools were expected to help people become effective employees and good citizens.

"Free schools" did not spread throughout the South until the Civil War ended in 1865. At that time, the newly freed black Americans had special problems. For generations, they had been enslaved and denied access to education. Now they had to overcome severe disadvantages arising from poverty, racism, and illiteracy.

Moreover, the Southern states had worse economic problems than other regions, even before the Civil War. After the War, the South had trouble funding schools, especially in rural areas. The region's prevailing ideas about the separation of blacks and whites led to a system in which each race attended its own schools.

Poor children in the cities had many disadvantages, too. Often, they worked ten to fourteen hours a day and did not attend school. Families needed the meager wages of these children, some only five or six years old, to survive. Children worked in canning factories and mills; they made artificial flowers and sewed kneepants in tenement "sweat shops." There was little time for rest, let alone for schooling.

INCREASING ROLES FOR SCHOOLS

As the 1900s arrived, thousands of new elementary schools and secondary schools were organized to meet a growing need for trained workers. In the cities, most children completed the eighth grade. The school year lengthened until it filled most of the calendar year.

Rural schools developed more slowly. One-room schoolhouses were still common in the early 1900s, and the school year was based upon the children's work schedule during planting and harvesting. The farm work schedule prompted schools to dismiss students every summer for a long vacation. Most U.S. schools have continued that schedule to the present day.

Gradually, all states made education compulsory—usually until a person reached the age of sixteen. All children now spent most months of the year attending school.

What were the goals of these schools and what should they teach? People debated the value of classical courses (a liberal arts education, including Greek and Latin) versus a more practical, industrial or trade-oriented education. Why should non-college-bound students learn trigonometry or Greek literature? asked those favoring the latter view. In many places, students could take a college-preparatory course, a vocational or business course, or a general course that included basic English, science, mathematics, geography, and history.

In *The Troubled Crusade*, Diane Ravitch, professor of history at Teachers College, Columbia University, points out that schools assumed more of the family's former roles. They now "had to meet young people's needs not only for education...but also for vocation, health, recreation, citizenship, and social competence."

After World War II, debates over federal aid for education intensified. The Senate Committee on Education and Labor held hearings to consider the economic inequalities that existed among the states and among individual school districts. During the Great Depression and World War I, the financial needs of many schools had been ignored. Now there were not enough teachers or textbooks, and teacher salaries were low. The situation was becoming critical. The NEA (National Education Association), NAACP (National Association for the Advancement of Colored People), and the PTA (National Parent-Teacher Association) were among those that advocated federal aid for schools. They believed the federal government should help local districts that lacked the money to fund schools adequately. Others opposed such aid. They argued that federal involvement might threaten the control that local people had traditionally exercised in their school districts.

Conflicts over aid to racially segregated schools and to parochial (primarily Catholic) schools stalled the passage of any substantial federal aid legislation. But the discussion had stirred public interest. Education became a standard political topic, linked to economics and other social issues.

In 1954 the U.S. Supreme Court ruled unanimously that states may not deliberately segregate public school children solely on the basis of race. Twenty-one states then had segregated school systems. Linda Brown of Topeka, Kansas, had been forced to attend a school twenty blocks from her home even though Sumner Elementary School—a "white" school—was only four blocks away. Her father and other parents sued the Board of Education in 1951, and the case of *Brown* v. *Board of Education of Topeka, Kansas* was decided three years later.

The Court held that such segregation violates the Constitution's Fourteenth Amendment, or Equal Protection Clause. The opinion of the Court said that separate facilities are inherently unequal and that forced segregation can lead to "a feeling of inferiority" among minority children.

Many people praised the *Brown* decision, saying that it supported the principles of justice and equal opportunity that the Constitution embodies. Critics, however, said that the decision violated state rights and individual rights. The decision was also criticized as being vague. The Court had told the states to desegregate their schools "with all deliberate speed," but states were left to determine individual plans and time frames.

Some cities, such as Louisville, Kentucky, desegregated their schools without much conflict. In other places—the Deep South states and, later, many northern cities—years of debate and protest followed the *Brown* decision.

When the Soviet Union launched the world's first space satellite, *Sputnik I*, in 1957, many Americans were alarmed that the U.S. education system was not producing enough top-notch scientists and technologists. Programs for gifted students were expanded to raise achievement levels in math and science, and foreign language skills were stressed.

But the 1960s became a period of social tumult. The civil rights movement, the feminist movement, political assassinations, and protests over the Vietnam War shifted the focus away from traditional views of education. There was unrest in large cities and on college campuses. In response to student demands, textbooks and curricula were changed to show the contributions of minorities and of women in America—material that had often been ignored. Students were given more choices of subjects, as schools tried to maintain their interest and keep the less academically inclined from dropping out.

CONCERNS IN THE 1980s

Were schools failing to set high enough expectations for performance? Were the graduation requirements too minimal? These were among the questions people asked during the 1980s as reports showed declining SAT scores and implied that U.S. students were not learning even basic material. Again, there was a call for educational "basics"; again, people were seeking the most effective ways to teach students, especially those at high risk of school failure.

Along with these issues, the schools found themselves facing increasing social problems: poverty, homelessness, child abuse, health problems, teenage pregnancy, drug abuse, and unstable families. School reform efforts during the 1980s were a response to these complex concerns. The goals set by President Bush and the states' governors address both the academic needs and some of the social problems that affect today's students.

What do people think about the six national education goals? Some critics say that the goals are not specific enough. Others ask how progress can be measured and by whom. Many people worry that there will be a lot of talk but little action.

An important concern is how the ambitious goals will be funded. In a *New York Times* interview in 1990, Keith Geiger, executive director of the National Education Association, said, "It's hard to disagree with anything they did. They still have not told us how they are going to pay for it." Addressing the governors, Speaker of the House of Representatives Thomas S. Foley questioned whether President Bush "can achieve that goal by proposing a meager 2 percent increase in federal spending on education.... we don't have a 2 percent education problem in this country. The education gap is much more daunting."

According to critics, many items need more funding, such as literacy projects, programs to prevent dropouts, child nutrition and preschool programs, and recruitment of qualified teachers. Such critics point out that the U.S. federal government contributes only 6 percent of the country's total education costs. Other countries pay more: For example, Japan's central government pays about 50 percent.

Other experts contend that poverty is a major cause of school problems, but it has not been fully addressed by the President or the governors. Harold Howe II, of the Harvard Graduate School of Education, says that the United States "can do a lot more with schools to be successful, but we can never get sufficiently successful when we have growing poverty in this country."

Students also express opinions about the education goals. "I don't know how we can become number one in science and math in just ten years," says one twelfth-grader. "At our school, we don't have a real physics teacher or a good science lab." A recent high school graduate who studied the goals as part of a course he took during his senior year says, "A lot of schools can't afford computers. A friend of mine goes to a school where the history books are out of date. The teacher has to keep bringing in maps for the class to use." A ninth-grader at an urban school comments, "Drugs are messing up kids at my school. It would be great if they could get rid of them, but everything they tried so far hasn't done much good."

Some students are concerned about the emphasis on evaluation, testing, and grades. "The grades don't always show what you learn. There are hard courses I would take, but I don't, because it might lower my grades," says a high school senior.

In spite of these misgivings, many people welcome the national debate and ongoing efforts to improve education. Ernest Boyer calls the process "a new affirmation of the work of the schools" and "a historic shift in the way this nation is willing to talk about the school agenda." And while Albert Shanker, president of the American Federation of Teachers (AFT), criticized several aspects of the national goals, he praised President Bush for "keeping education at the top of the national agenda," and said, "Now that we have [the national goals] we need to look at them, discuss them widely and rework them where they need it. There's too much at stake not to do it right."

CHAPTER THREE

LANGUAGE

SKILLS AND

LITERACY

WHAT should people learn and how should it be taught? This important question has been raised in different reports on education and by people who want to change school curricula. In considering a basic curriculum for American students, most people start with the "3 Rs": reading, writing, and arithmetic. The first "R," reading, is regarded as the foundation for other learning, a skill that every capable person should master.

"I guess I should read more," says a fourteen-year-old from Indiana. "I don't seem to have much free time. When I do, I watch TV more than I read."

"We read so much in school," says a high school junior living in Connecticut. "When I get home, I'd rather be outside or do something relaxing."

Some people blame the lack of reading on television's influence. A high school English teacher told of a student in his class who read only a few chapters of every assigned book, explaining, "I can't read your books because I've got my programs to watch." Another student told him she was "hooked" on television, especially soap operas.

Aside from its value in helping a person to get a job and then to advance in a career, reading is needed for many common tasks: understanding utility bills, bank statements, maps, warning labels, signs, and other instructions; filling out forms for job applications, income taxes, and bank loans; finding out about world and local news; making informed decisions as a voter.

People who cannot read and understand written messages are more vulnerable to the opinions and pressures of others. They may not develop the reasoning skills needed to judge messages from other people and from the media.

Nonreaders also miss out on the pleasure and variety of experiences that reading offers. A person who recently learned to read with the help of a library literacy program described the joy of going into a library, walking out with an armful of books, then spending hours reading a spine-tingling mystery or adventure story. Another graduate of that program said that she had become a "biography nut." Human history and culture and universal emotions can be found inside the covers of books.

Despite widespread agreement about the importance of reading, statistics from the U.S. Department of Education show that many Americans cannot read and comprehend well or even at all. About 30 million are functionally illiterate (lack skills above fourth-grade level).

In its *Reading Report Card* (1985), the Education Department found that 40 percent of the nation's thirteen-year-olds and 16 percent of the seventeen-year-olds did not have intermediate reading skills (i.e., they could not find key information, link and compare ideas, or generalize, using materials in science, literature, or social studies). Only 5 percent of the seventeen-year-olds tested had advanced reading skills—the kind needed to understand complex ideas found in professional or technical journals and textbooks.

Another study, *Workforce 2000: Work and Workers for the 21st Century,* concluded that people aged twenty-one to twenty-five read at a level lower than that needed for the average job in the mid-1980s. On a scale of 0–6, the average reading level of these adults is about 2.6—below the 3.0 level needed for America's current 105,000,000 nonmilitary jobs (e.g., retail salesperson or construction worker) and well below the 3.6 level that will be needed for most jobs by the year 2000. Highly skilled professionals in scientific fields must read at a much higher level: 6.0.

VITAL ROLES FOR SCHOOLS AND PARENTS

What methods help people learn to read? The phonics method has been used for years, and many educators still use this approach, which stresses the connection between sounds and letters, as the learner sounds out unfamiliar words. Research is being done to determine the effectiveness of other methods, as well as to see how different ways of teaching reading suit the needs of different learners.

Researchers also emphasize the important role that parents and other adults in a child's environment play in fostering a love of reading. Parents are urged to read to their children from the time they are babies. Reading and talking to a child, say these researchers, will increase the child's verbal skills and later academic success.

A 1987 government study said that, on average, American mothers "spend less than half an hour a day talking, explaining, or reading things with their children," and fathers spend even less time—about fifteen minutes. In many cases, there is only one parent in the home or both parents hold full-time jobs, so they spend much time at home doing household chores. Other parents claim that they did not realize how important it is to read with their children. And in many homes, watching television replaces reading and conversation.

Fourth-graders in Pennsylvania read up on ecology in a natural environment—a classroom bathtub.

Besides reading, parents can do other important things, according to the research. They can visit the public library regularly and keep books and magazines available in the home, providing a "print-rich" environment. They can discuss the stories they read with a child and those that the child reads alone. Such discussions can help children make connections between written words, ideas, and personal and social values.

Later, independent reading by the child assumes increasing importance. The amount of time spent reading correlates with a child's vocabulary size, comprehension, and overall school achievement. Yet the Center for the Study of Reading found that a typical fifth-grader watches TV more than two hours a day, but reads for an average of only four minutes per day.

Some educators and researchers recommend that more classroom time be allocated for silent reading. They urge that every school maintain a library and that every classroom contain its own shelves of books. They also recommend that beginning readers use materials that hold their interest, not drab, repetitious exercises. Short chapter books with well-developed plots and characters are now available for beginning readers.

Many educators worry that students do not read enough top-quality literature—classics—either in or out of school. They recommend that schools identify these literary works and make them part of every student's education.

"I didn't think I would like reading *A Tale of Two Cities*, by Charles Dickens, but I did," says a high school sophomore. "The experiences of the characters in the book reminded me of things that my friends and I are going through, growing up."

Unfortunately, many Americans have no access to the classics or to any literature: They cannot read.

PROMOTING ADULT LITERACY

The issue of adult literacy is important for many reasons, including its impact upon children. An illiterate adult cannot be a reading role model for a child.

Adult education programs throughout the nation are addressing this problem, aided by Literacy Volunteers of America (LVOA) and state and local organizations that help people learn to read. During the 1980s, the Vermont Department of Education got a head start on the national goal of "total literacy by the year 2000" when it set that goal for its own state. To teach an estimated 58,000 adult citizens how to read, the Vermont Reading Project has been working with local Adult Basic Education Programs and the Vermont Council on the Humanities.

In October 1989, Vermont held a statewide literacy conference, inviting illiterate and formerly illiterate adults to participate. Participant Ed MacAuley, a former factory worker who graduated from high school unable to read or write, offered this advice to public schools: "Put all your money, all your best teachers, into the first six grades. No one should leave sixth grade without learning how to read." In 1985, Mr. MacAuley learned to read during an Adult Education course. Now he has a new job and is enjoying books for the first time.

Throughout America, volunteers and public agencies are helping people learn to read. Many public libraries conduct literacy programs. At the Brooklyn Public Library in New York City, more than 2,500 nonreading adults and unemployed young people were learning to read in early 1990, working individually with volunteer tutors, on computers, or in small study groups.

Literacy Volunteers of America sponsors many programs. The skill level of adults enrolled in such programs varies widely. Some need help with comprehension and thinking skills; others have not yet mastered the alphabet. Tutors work one-on-one with students, basing their approach on the student's needs.

The U.S. Congress has recognized the need to coordinate existing literacy programs and to fund some new ones. The Adult Literacy and Employability bill (H.R. 3123), introduced in 1989, aims to increase funding to fight illiteracy and to coordinate adult, family, and work-force programs. The bill would establish a Cabinet council and national and state literacy resource centers and give financial aid to state programs that help people learn to speak English. It would also fund library literacy pilot programs.

AN ESSENTIAL JOB FOR SCHOOLS

What if a child has difficulty in learning to read? Perhaps the family members are unwilling or unable to help or cannot speak English. Teacher/author Herbert Kohl says that the public school still has a duty to teach every able child to read: "Since reading is basic in our society, it's important to find a way to enable that person to read....if X can't read, we have to figure out, with the help of X, how to help him get power over the written word....It's a simple matter of fitting learning and teaching together." In *High School*, Ernest Boyer agrees and says that "Language development of each child should be carefully monitored....If a student is not making satisfactory progress, special tutoring should be provided."

Kohl points out that in the past, programs were developed to teach immigrants and other nonliterate adults to read and write, despite poverty and other problems that these people often faced. The same commitment must be made today, he says.

That kind of commitment has helped children like Erik R., a fifth-grader who attends a school in the Bronx section of New York City. In fourth grade, he struggled to read at the first-grade level. But summer school and the help of a reading resource teacher in his school have enabled him to master words like "comprehensive" and "hierophant." These are two of "Erik's words." He writes words like these, along with their definitions, on index cards, then keeps the cards in a file box under his name. His reading teacher, Louise Warren, uses the cards to help her students realize that they can learn large, unfamiliar words. One of her goals is to help students believe in themselves through success in reading and speaking. "These children can do the work if you give them the time," says Mrs. Warren.

LITERACY ADVOCATES

Literacy is receiving even more attention during the 1990s because it is a long-standing interests of First Lady Barbara Bush. Mrs. Bush has been a volunteer in the Reading Is Fundamental (RIF) program, which encourages children to read and distributes free books for them to keep. She has visited hundreds of literacy programs. During public appearances at schools and libraries, she stresses literacy for all Americans. Mrs. Bush has said, "I thought about all the things that seemed important to me, and I realized that everything I worry about would be better if everyone could read, write, and comprehend."

Mrs. Bush is the honorary chairperson of a private foundation to promote literacy. The Barbara Bush Foundation for Family

First Lady Barbara Bush frequently visits schools and libraries to promote reading and literacy programs.

Literacy will distribute funds donated by foundations, corporations, and individuals. The foundation focuses upon family-centered efforts to fight illiteracy. Mrs. Bush is convinced that "we must attack the problem of a more literate America through the family. We all know that adults with reading problems tend to raise children with reading problems." Thus the Barbara Bush Foundation will develop family literacy programs, support volunteer training, and help ongoing programs to add inter-generational activities.

At the same time, UNESCO (United Nations Educational Scientific and Cultural Organization) named 1990 as International Literacy Year. It launched a ten-year effort to promote worldwide literacy, beginning with a 1990 world conference in Bangkok.

Worldwide, efforts for literacy are based upon the belief that people need access to information, as well as the ability to ask questions and express ideas in our increasingly communication-oriented world. Reading and writing are indeed basic tools.

WRITING: ANOTHER BASIC

Writing—in a clear, grammatical way—is linked with reading as a basic skill, especially because today's world presents increasing numbers of jobs in communication-related fields.

In January 1990, Education Secretary Lauro F. Cavazos held a news conference to discuss the results of a national assessment of reading and writing skills. Secretary Cavazos called the results "dreadfully inadequate," stating that "as a nation, we should be appalled that we have placed our children in such jeopardy. Reading and writing are the basic tools of learning, the crux of the academic enterprise."

Many teachers complain that they do not have time to read and grade as many essay tests or term papers as they would like. Mary Futrell, former president of the National Education Association, has said that crowded classrooms often lead teachers to use multiple-choice or true-false tests, which take less time to grade, instead of essay tests.

A history teacher teacher in a suburban high school in North Carolina described his situation: "Here, teachers are assigned to about 140 students a day, with only an hour period for clerical work, lesson planning, and grading." The teacher described the extra weekends and nights he spent grading term papers written by 142 students. "I can't read them as thoughtfully as I'd like. It takes about two and a half hours just to evaluate the mechanics, like footnotes or bibliographical information, and to correct the major errors in spelling and grammar. I don't have enough time to make specific comments about the overall style and details in the writing. It's frustrating."

What methods help students learn the writing skills they need in order to communicate ideas clearly? In 1986, *What Works: Research About Teaching and Learning,* a report by the U.S. Department of Education, stressed the importance of frequent practice in writing, using a four-step process of "brainstorming, composing, revising, editing." It also urged that students write more during their other courses.

The idea of integrating writing into the rest of the curriculum is not new, but it has been gaining attention. "There's an increasing call for whole faculties—not just English teachers, but also science and math teachers—to use writing as a way for kids to not just retain materials, but to understand it and make it their own," says Mary Ann Smith, a junior high school English teacher who directs the Bay Area Writing Project in San Francisco. This project, conducts summer sessions to help teachers use writing in different subjects. It became a model for the National Writing Project, which now trains about 80,000 U.S. teachers each year at more than 165 locations.

Some schools bring professional writers into the classroom to work with students. Authors may visit for one day or spend more time at the school as a "writer-in-residence," helping students to improve their writing. In one North Carolina school a fourth-grade teacher told of increased student interest in both reading and writing after an author's weeklong visit: "The students were inspired by meeting a 'real author.' They spent extra time in the library looking for the author's books and for books that the author mentioned in her discussions. Several students volunteered to write for the school newsletter."

In *Writing to Learn,* William Zinsser says that students should write in every course in the school curriculum, because writing helps us to learn: "Writing is how we think our way into a subject and make it our own. Writing enables us to find out what we know—and what we don't know—about whatever we're trying to learn."

WRITING SKILLS REQUIRED

Jobs in the future will require more writing and communication skills than did the manufacturing jobs of the past. Today's jobs commonly require the writing of clear, logical business letters and memos, often on a daily basis. Yet Diane Capstaff, vice president for corporate services at John Hancock Mutual Life Insurance Company in Boston, has discovered that many applicants "don't have the writing skills to prepare a brief letter to a policy holder."

Employers describe letters and memos that contain spelling errors (like "sincerly" and "attendence") and errors in grammar. Furthermore, some employees do not use words correctly and cannot construct logical sentences and paragraphs.

Writing tests are being added to applications for some jobs and for admission to colleges and professional schools. In spring 1989, the Association of American Medical Colleges said that it will include a test of writing skills in examinations taken by students who apply to medical schools.

If this trend continues, schools throughout the United States may see an even greater need for programs that help students learn to write well. And the goal of total literacy by the year 2000 will get a needed boost, as reading and writing become national priorities.

CHAPTER FOUR

PREPARATION FOR

A CHANGING WORLD:

SCIENCE, MATH,

AND TECHNOLOGY

"**W**HY should I learn this stuff?" a high school freshman says, pointing to her biology textbook. "I want to be a graphic artist. I don't need to know all this science."

"Chemistry is a waste of time," says a high school junior. "What difference will it ever make in my life if I know about atoms and molecules?"

A number of people are worried about comments like these. They say that America needs strong science education not only to train top-notch scientists and engineers, but also because of the growing need for *all* citizens to understand science.

Why do citizens need a basic education in science? "Average citizens" may help to define public policy about controversial diseases like AIDS or about the ethical uses of new medical technology. They will elect legislators who decide what kinds of scientific research should be funded. Citizens must help to decide how the federal government and local communities will handle environmental problems. People without scientific literacy "are foreigners in their own country," says Paul DeHart Hurd, professor of science education at Stanford University. Without a basic science background, we cannot understand or debate scientific issues, much less make informed decisions as voters. This leaves decisions affecting all of us to small groups of science "experts" or to politicians.

As well as informed citizens, we need scientists and technologists who can use their expertise for research and development. In setting a national goal in 1989 that U.S. students will become "first in science and mathematics," the President and governors expressed their concern that America will not be competitive enough in global markets unless it remains strong in technology. Other people fear that, if that happens, the U.S. standard of living and its influence in the world could decline.

International studies show American students lagging behind others. In a comparison of thirteen-year-olds from fourteen countries and Canadian provinces, U.S. students ranked at or near the bottom in every category. Ninth-graders placed thirteenth out of fourteen in general science knowledge. Twelfth-grade chemistry students finished twelfth out of fourteen, behind Australia, Japan, Singapore, and others.

Performance in mathematics is also disappointing. The NCEE report *A Nation at Risk* said that remedial mathematics courses in universities rose by 72 percent between 1975 and 1980. Top U.S. students continue to score as well as top students from other but they are only about 10 percent of the total.

Some people criticize international comparisons, calling them inaccurate, misleading, or both. Roald Hoffmann, a 1981 Nobel laureate in chemistry and professor of physical science at Cornell University, says, "Surveys that plumb the depths of our ignorance and that of our students are methodologically suspect...' More importantly, the interpretation of these statistics in isolation is questionable. One needs an accompanying discussion of the social, cultural, and economic environment in which these supposedly ignorant individuals function in ... society." He also points out that America faces a unique challenge because of its "heterogeneous population, with immigrants from hundreds of cultures, from incredibly divergent family structures ... "

Teacher LeRoy E. Hay cautions Americans against an emphasis on being "first" in everything, compared to other nations. "Could it be that the 'have-nots' are catching up with the 'haves' and we don't like it?" he asks. "Could it be that we cannot face being second or even tied for first?"

But many people think that at least some test results are a cause for concern. Diane Ravitch contends that recent science and math surveys were given to similar populations and that, in some cases, "It was our best students, not our average students, who scored so poorly." The surveys, claims Ravitch, show "real deficiencies in our educational system. We are not helped to address those deficiencies by rationalizing them away."

REASONS FOR LOWER ACHIEVEMENT

What are some of the factors that result in lower science achievement? Some people mention an attitude problem, or what *Newsweek* magazine in 1990 called the "nerd factor." Stephen Jay Gould, biology professor at Harvard, remembers that when he attended school, "any kid with a passionate interest in science was a wonk, a square, a dweeb, a doofus, or a geek." Some teenagers think that science and scientists are dull and that a science career will not bring wealth or fame—things which are valued by the larger society.

In *The Schools We Deserve*, Diane Ravitch faults the lowering of graduation requirements and expectations of students. She says that while highly motivated students have continued to take challenging, college-preparatory courses, average and below-average students—"who might have learned more if the expectations of the school had been clear and consistent"—often avoid courses that seem too demanding.

Educator Albert Shanker points out another aspect of the problem: a shortage of qualified science and mathematics teachers in elementary and secondary schools. Shanker cites statistics from the National Science Teachers Association that show 80 percent of high school science teachers are teaching outside their primary field and almost one-third of the nation's high school physics teachers never took a physics course.

Furthermore, says Shanker, high school students use textbooks written by people who "assume—correctly—that students are unlikely to have learned any science in elementary school. No wonder they do so miserably compared with thirteen-year-olds from other countries." As for math, Shanker claims that the U.S. is the only industrialized country "where you can graduate from high school and college without knowing much beyond arithmetic."

Scott Thomson, director of the National Association of Secondary School Principals, found other potential reasons for lower science achievement. Thomson studied habits of thirteen-year-olds in different countries and found that 71 percent of South Korean students often watch science programs on TV. Only 37 percent of U.S. thirteen-year-olds do—the lowest rate of all the groups studied. Thomson also notes that many U.S. students work after school and on weekends in order to buy things they see in TV ads that feature consumer goods for teenagers. The South Korean students in the study did not work during school months; the West Germans seldom worked, except to help out in a family business.

Does employment hurt school achievement? This is an important issue for students and families. Research shows that when students work more than fifteen hours a week during school months, their grades may fall. One teenager explains, "I was working weekends and some nights at a restaurant. The other people were finished with school, and two of them had dropped out. They would ask me to play basketball or go out at night. They didn't have to worry about school or homework." Socializing with people who are not involved with school can lower a student's own interest in schoolwork. Fatigue may also be a problem. A seventeen-year-old who worked from two-thirty until eleven o'clock at a supermarket on weekdays says, "By the time I got home, I really didn't do my homework."

Teenagers must think carefully about what type of job and how many hours they should work during school weeks.

A SHORTAGE OF SCIENCE STUDENTS

The American Council on Education states that college enrollments in science courses are at an all-time low. In 1973, 11.5 percent of entering college freshmen planned to major in science and math; by 1989, it was down to 5.8 percent.

Educators believe that talented students who might study science and engineering now prefer the higher salaries offered by business careers. "They want their M.B.A.'s. They want to make fast money," said Professor Babu George, director of science and math at Sacred Heart University in Fairfield, Connecticut. Dr. George said that only four or five chemistry degrees, five or six biology degrees, and two or three math degrees are awarded annually at his campus—"And this is the national average."

"I started as a chemistry major," says a college sophomore at a large midwestern university. "The lab courses took three afternoons a week and Saturday mornings. There was more homework—harder homework—than what I get in my other courses. And I have to work part-time."

Other students express similar concerns, saying that they do not major in science or math because these subjects are difficult and require so much study. The National Science Foundation found that 40 percent of the college freshmen who plan to pursue science careers drop out after taking just one course. By graduation, 60 percent have changed fields.

The foundation estimates that by 2000, the U.S. will have a shortage of 430,000 scientists and engineers with bachelor's degrees. And there is a shortage of science teachers at every level.

IMPROVING SCIENCE EDUCATION

Efforts are being made to increase America's supply of scientists and science teachers and to increase scientific knowledge among the general public. More time spent studying science is recommended by many groups. The National Science Board Commission advocates that students in grades K–6 devote at least one hour per day to math and thirty minutes per day to science.

High schools should require at least two, preferably three, science courses. In many industrialized countries, all students study biology, chemistry, physics, and advanced mathematics. Many study both mathematics and science during all four years of high school. Only 1 percent of American students take calculus, compared to 12 percent of Japan's students.

The National Science Board Commission recommends ways to improve science, mathematics, and technology education. In *Educating Americans for the Twenty-first Century,* the board outlines a comprehensive program that begins in kindergarten and progresses in a well-planned way through high school, building upon concepts and skills.

What methods of teaching science work best? Experts have criticized the exclusive use of more traditional methods— lecturing, reading, and memorizing. University of Chicago professor Leon Lederman, who won a 1988 Nobel Prize in physics, says bluntly that many science programs discourage children's natural interest "and manage to beat the curiosity right out of them." Dr. Carlo Parvanno, professor at the State University of New York at Purchase, calls children "born

Most science educators favor a "hands-on" approach, such as dissecting a frog, to learn about anatomy and physiology.

scientists" but warns that "if students don't have a positive attitude toward science by the third or fourth grade, chances are we have lost them."

Many experts favor a "hands-on" approach to science education, with an emphasis on experiments—"science in action." Some American schools have replaced textbooks with experiment kits. Experiments help students to ask scientific questions and then test their theories, seeing the evidence for themselves.

As they search for effective ways to teach science, educators stress the many benefits of studying the sciences. A logical approach to problem-solving improves thinking, as students learn to separate their opinions and assumptions from facts. In *First Lessons: A Report on Elementary Education in America,* former Education Secretary William J. Bennett wrote, "The scientific method is the method of thought, of reasoning, which applies not only to exploration of the physical universe but to all realms of intellectual inquiry that require hypothesis, inference, and other tools of brainwork." Efforts to improve science achievement also focus on the need for improvement in mathematics.

A GOOD START IN MATHEMATICS

"I'm terrible at math," says an eighth-grader. "It's my worst subject." According to educators, students like this one may be far more capable than they realize. But they suffer from a lack of enthusiasm and perhaps "math anxiety."

Yet the National Science Board Commission says that young children have an "innate number sense." It recommends that mathematics education aim to "develop confidence and minimize 'math anxiety.'" The Commission also advises getting rid of excess drill, which students may find boring and irrelevant.

What are the alternatives to math drills? Many experts cite the value of "manipulatives"—objects such as buttons, coins, beads, or cards—that children can use to visualize mathematical concepts. Students work with such objects in order to move from concrete to abstract reasoning.

Educators disagree about how much time should be spent on drills. Textbook author John Saxon says that in the early grades, drills using pencil and paper provide important practice and are the "building-blocks" of later success in math. Schools are looking for the best combination of drills and activities, especially in the lower grades, to provide a basis for higher-level skills. By the ninth grade, says the Science Board Commission, students should have skill with word problems, percentages, estimates, elementary statistics, simple geometry, fractions and decimals, concepts of sets, and beginning algebra.

"I guess my problem is that I got behind last year," says a ninth-grade student who is failing his math course. "I missed something along the way, and now none of it seems to make sense." Without finding ways to catch up, such students don't progress to higher-level skills, much less to the math needed for certain jobs.

The "math of tomorrow"—skills that people will need in the future—involves critical thinking and the ability to apply mathematics. In 1989 the National Council of Teachers of Mathematics recommended that teachers emphasize reasoning and the use of math to solve real-world problems. Students still need basic mechanical skills, said the council, but they must think, read, write, and speak the "language of mathematics." Said council president Shirley M. Frye, "Students are not computing machines. They are thinking machines."

In order to improve math skills and prepare students for the future, some schools have made dramatic changes, such as integrating different disciplines—trigonometry, geometry, algebra, and calculus—instead of separating them into year-long courses. Mathematics history is also getting more attention. Experts say that math becomes far more interesting to students when the creative history and the people who developed mathematics are discussed in classes and textbooks.

During the 1980s, schools in Dobbs Ferry, New York, changed their math programs to reflect some of these new ideas. Math courses are blended with other subjects—social sciences, "pure" sciences, and business. Students may use math to analyze voting trends, devise routes for delivery trucks, and predict business profits. One senior who transferred to the Dobbs Ferry school from another town comments, "I enjoy math more than I did before, and my grades have improved this past year."

COMPUTER LITERACY

Preparing students to cope with today's workplace and with changes in technology requires computer literacy, say the experts. The National Science Board states that all students should understand how computers work. They should know basic terminology and at least one high-level computer language. Students should master word processing and filing systems and use a computer language to do problem-solving tasks for different courses.

There are 9.5 million personal computers in schools and colleges, compared to 600,000 in 1982. How can they be used most effectively? Herbert Kohl warns against using computers merely for mechanical purposes, such as drills, lest they become no more than expensive "flash cards."

Kohl says that children can benefit in many ways by playing computer games, if the games are complex, activity-oriented, and keep children mentally alert. "I didn't like any kind of math until I did it on the computer," says a sixth-grader. Another student describes her newfound interest in geography after using a computer program that teaches it in a colorful way. "Computers give the children more self-confidence," says a middle-school math teacher. "They enjoy being able to handle the machine. They think it is more fun than work."

Educators stress the need to help teachers learn to use computers effectively. To that end, many teachers attend special training sessions. Linda G. Roberts, of the Congressional Office of Technology Assessment, agrees that "if we are concerned about keeping teachers up to date in their fields, improving their classroom management skills and helping them assume new instructional strategies in the restructuring of education, we must give them the tools they need."

Do American schools have enough computers? In a 1989 survey, Henry Jay Becker, project director of the Center for Social Organization of Schools at Johns Hopkins University, found an average ratio of one computer to every twenty students. But this ratio can differ greatly, depending upon the school district. When the New Jersey Supreme Court studied the number of computers in schools, it found that in Princeton, a wealthy district, there was one computer per eight children. But cities with less money for schools, such as Camden, had only one computer for fifty-eight children.

Becker also studied how computers are used in schools. He found that students spend 50 percent of their computer time learning to use the keyboard and the various writing, filing, and accounting programs. Critics would like students to spend more time with innovative techniques in instruction. But limited numbers of machines mean students often work with computers in groups, rather than individually.

In addition, computers function as labor-saving devices in the schools. Teacher time can be saved when computers are used to average grades or when students use computers to learn math or grammar rules, for example. Many people contend that education cannot be automated as much as some other areas because of the nature of the student-teacher relationship. Nonetheless, computers offer students and teachers powerful new tools for learning. They may help students toward higher achievement in many subject areas, including science and mathematics.

GENERATING ENTHUSIASM

As the twenty-first century draws near, how can schools encourage students to develop a strong interest in science and mathematics, as well as to understand why these subjects are important both for the nation and for individuals?

An Ohio educator who has taught a popular science course to eighth-grade students for thirty-five years expresses concern that during that time, no student teachers majoring in science have come to his school. Yet he says that his profession is tremendously rewarding: "I am just as excited about teaching science this year as I was when I started thirty-five years ago. Although I have changed the material in the course through the years, I have not changed my approach to teaching—student-centered with hands-on learning. I think students should have fun studying science. My reward comes from seeing students enjoy learning and, later, from watching them become educated, productive adults." One answer to America's "science gap" may well lie in finding more teachers who share this man's enthusiasm for helping students to learn.

CHAPTER FIVE

CITIZENS IN
A LARGER WORLD:
SOCIAL STUDIES AND
FOREIGN LANGUAGES

"IN today's world, if you don't know where you are, you are nowhere," declared Gilbert Grosvenor, president of the National Geographic Society. Grosvenor was referring to reports that say Americans don't know much about the world around them. In one 1987 survey, 45 percent of high school seniors in Baltimore could not locate the United States on a world map; 40 percent of those in Kansas City could not list three South American countries; 39 percent in Boston did not know the names of the six New England states—the states that make up their own region.

Geography, history, civics, and current events are included in the subject area called "social studies." Experts say that U.S. students are not learning enough about any of these subjects.

Lloyd H. Elliot, president of George Washington University, notes that during the 1940s and 1950s geography was made part

Students at the Nathan Hale Intermediate School in Brooklyn, New York, make papier-mâché globes to track trade routes.

of a general and integrated curriculum in social sciences rather than remaining a separate subject. As a result, says Elliot, "geography was lost... it disappeared in elementary and secondary schools [and also] in the college curricula, because there weren't professors being trained to teach geography." Since the trend changed in the 1970s, he says, "we have been struggling to catch up."

Geography is more than identifying countries and cities on a map, say its supporters. According to Elliot, "We must all understand the physical and cultural dynamics of the earth if we are to be responsible citizens of the world.... Through geography learners of all ages can see the importance of other languages, literature, the arts, mathematics, music, and religion—in fact, the world's knowledge."

But students often identify geography as one of their "least favorite subjects." One fourteen-year-old says, "The geography book is boring. It just tells things like what crops grow in this place and where mountains and rivers are.... I'd rather learn more about how the people live, not just the climate."

As is true for other disciplines, better geography instruction requires better-qualified teachers. Seeing this need, the National Geographic Society established a new education foundation in 1988. Using donated funds and bequests, the foundation supports quality geography education in the United States. Some of the money is being devoted to teacher training throughout America. At annual institutes in such places as northern California, teachers share new materials and techniques that they can use in the classroom.

GAPS IN KNOWLEDGE OF HISTORY

Just as some tests indicate that Americans lack geographic literacy, other tests show gaps in knowledge of history and current events. In 1988, ABC News broadcast a television special with the unflattering title "America's Kids: Why They Flunk." In its assessment of two hundred high school seniors, the survey team found that most students could identify pop singers Michael Jackson and Madonna. But most could not identify historical figures, such as Lenin, or modern leaders like Daniel Ortega and Fidel Castro.

If it is true that those who do not understand history are doomed to repeat it, then many of today's students are at risk. Research by the National Center for Education Statistics found that students do not study history as often or as extensively as past generations of Americans or students in other countries.

During the 1960s and 1970s requirements were lowered in many high schools. Students could graduate after taking one course in American history and perhaps one other social studies course. Some states required just one course—American history.

Analyzing how history courses are actually taught, the U.S. Department of Education found that many students do not get experience in writing research papers or identifying and using original source materials. They do not perform tasks that develop skills in "reasoning...such as evaluating sources of information, drawing conclusions, and constructing logical arguments," according to *What Works: Research About Teaching and Learning*.

Such reports have led educators like Albert Shanker to ask, "How can we expect our future citizens to appreciate the birth of democracy abroad when they do not understand its history and significance at home?"

IMPROVING ACHIEVEMENT

What can be done to improve student achievement in these subjects? In *A Nation at Risk*, the NCEE recommends that schools must require more demanding course work and more hours of study and homework, and they must set stricter graduation requirements.

Students and educators have expressed concern about textbooks, too. After studying high school history texts, the American Federation of Teachers described many books as "bland." AFT researchers said that some books omit vital information about historical figures and that they do not give enough attention to economics, religion, and the role of women and minorities in America's past.

The author of the AFT study, Paul Gagnon, a history professor at the University of Massachusetts, said that the textbooks "are not awful. They're not wrong. But they just don't offer enough help to teachers when we're facing increasingly complex problems in a diverse world." He criticized the numerous graphics and special features that take space away from details and analyses that could stimulate thoughtful classroom debates.

Other people call for an integrated approach to world history and a curriculum that shows the importance of non-European (or non-Western) civilizations. Donald Johnson, professor of international education at New York University, says that people whose ancestry is not European would then have "the chance to see their own historical traditions as a genuine part of world civilization and not simply as exotic deviations from the 'rise of the West.'"

But the companies that produce textbooks face obstacles in carrying out some of these recommendations. Pressure from parents and some special-interest groups such as the conservative Moral Majority have influenced some publishers to avoid certain controversial issues. As a result, many textbook publishers try to avoid offending various people, and the books have been "watered down," say many educators.

In teaching current events—the "history" that is happening right now—educators face different challenges. It is impossible for textbooks to keep up with events that are taking place day by day. In an effort to help students understand the rapid changes in Eastern Europe and many other regions of the world, teachers must be resourceful. Many of them devise creative new approaches, often relying on daily newspapers, magazines, and television news programs as material for classroom discussions.

Some teachers complain that students are indifferent to world events, that they call history "boring" and see no reason to learn it. A teacher in a New York public school thinks that there are some valid reasons for this situation. He points out that growing up in a "global village makes it difficult for kids to identify with people. The spelling is so different. The names are difficult. It is more difficult to teach kids than a few years ago."

Students complain that, in many cases, their history studies seem "irrelevant." If so, then the challenge to teachers, textbook authors, and others is to help students understand the impact of history and current events. A contest—the National Geography Bee—has helped to motivate some students. Students from different cities compete in regional bees. State regional winners compete in Washington, D.C., where they answer questions about geography, history, and current events.

Computers are also increasing interest in geography and history. Students can use games that offer information along with illustrations and quizzes that test their knowledge. The

Apple Global Education Network gives students a chance to share ideas and information with students living in other cities, as well as different countries, by way of a satellite network that links schools in North America, Europe, and the Middle East.

Students describe the excitement of sending questions or messages and receiving answers from fellow students in other lands. "I was amazed how well the German students can speak English," says a ninth-grader. "It made me more interested in foreign languages."

FOREIGN LANGUAGES: A NEW BASIC?

The importance of speaking foreign languages and understanding other cultures is more evident than ever. The world continues to shrink with faster transportation and means of communication. Trade occurs among more nations. In 1989 and 1990, major changes took place in Eastern Europe. The Berlin Wall between East and West Germany "fell," and the Iron Curtain seemed to disappear within weeks as Hungary opened its borders and new governments were established in Poland and Czechoslovakia.

Changes are also continuing to occur here in America. Our population has changed many times as immigrants from different places settled in particular regions. In Los Angeles, 62 percent of the students in the Los Angeles Unified Public School District are Hispanic. By 2030, it is estimated that 35 to 40 percent of the population of California will be Hispanic. There are more Puerto Ricans living in New York City than in San Juan. Asian immigrants live in many U.S. cities. Large U.S. companies have been purchased by foreign investors.

Yet most Americans cannot speak any language except English fluently. "I've taken German for two years," says a high school senior. "A friend of mine had relatives visiting from Austria, and I thought I could talk with them in German. But I speak too slowly, and I couldn't keep up with them. I probably could have worked harder in class and spent more time reviewing each night. But a big problem is that I just don't get to use the language much. I almost forgot what I learned last year, over the summer."

Except for Spanish, many Americans are rarely exposed to a foreign language and culture, whereas in Europe, countries are smaller and closer to other nations with different languages. In Switzerland, German, French, and Italian are all spoken within its borders. Many Europeans, Africans, and Asians speak two or three languages, including English, fluently.

The situation is quite different in the United States, where many people do not learn foreign languages either through interaction with non-English speaking people or in school. The number of U.S. students enrolled in foreign language courses declined after the early 1900s. In 1979 only 15 percent of all high school students studied a foreign language. During the 1980s this trend was reversed as some states began to require foreign language study. But even where languages are encouraged or required, many students do not start until high school, and they may study the language for only one or two years.

In the United States economics may determine whether a school can offer foreign languages before high school. When the New Jersey Supreme Court examined differences in education among rich and poor school districts, it found that in wealthier districts, foreign language study began anywhere from preschool to fifth grade. Less affluent districts offered the courses starting in tenth grade. Yet research says people learn new languages best when they begin in the early grades—preferably before age ten. Indeed, some research suggests that the ability to learn a new language decreases sharply by the teenage years.

Furthermore, experts urge that a child study the same language for six to eight years. They advocate combining language study with activities like cooking or games and say that academic subjects should be taught bilingually.

What will increase America's foreign language skills as we

move toward the year 2000? We need more qualified teachers in both primary and secondary schools. But between 1970 and 1985, there was a 53 percent decrease in the number of foreign language degrees awarded. Raising foreign language requirements and increasing the number of courses may not be enough to motivate students, unless they see the importance of their studies. One valuable resource may be students themselves. Bilingual children attend many U.S. schools. They might help other children use the languages they are learning in the classroom to communicate in other settings, such as the playground, gym, or music class. This would make the new languages more meaningful.

Educators are encouraged by the growing popularity of foreign language courses. Between 1982 and 1985, the number of students in grades seven through twelve taking foreign language courses increased by more than one million. Texas, Florida, and New York report impressive 50 percent gains in enrollment. The American Council on the Teaching of Foreign Languages has followed these trends and stresses the need to maintain student interest in foreign language study by skillful teaching that emphasizes conversational skills.

Foreign languages and a strong social studies curriculum have a central place in today's schools, say the experts. Today, more than ever before, people from many countries are uniting to solve common problems, such as alleviating hunger and malnutrition, protecting the environment, and preventing nuclear war. Education plays a vital role in helping all of us to see "the big picture" and to understand the interdependent nature of today's world.

CHAPTER SIX

WHAT ELSE

SHOULD SCHOOLS

TEACH?

THROUGH the years schools have aimed to promote personal health, social skills, and citizenship. They offer many courses besides those in English, math, science, social studies, foreign languages, and computer science. Such courses can vary greatly from one school to another, and some—such as drug and sex education—are controversial.

In *Basic Skills*, Herbert Kohl lists six skills that he thinks are important for all Americans:

1. the ability to use language well and thoughtfully

2. the ability to think through a problem and experiment with solutions

3. the ability to understand scientific and technological ideas and to use tools

Arts education often falls victim to budget cuts, but corporate grants sometimes help finance such programs. The RJR Nabisco Foundation paid for this school band's musical instruments.

4. the ability to use the imagination and participate in and appreciate different forms of personal and group expression

5. the ability to understand how people function in groups and to apply that knowledge to group problems in one's own life

6. the ability to know how to learn something yourself and to have the skills and confidence to be a learner all your life

THE ROLE OF ARTS EDUCATION

In discussing the fourth skill, Kohl recommends that "serious attention be given to the arts from historical, performance, and technical aspects." Author/educator Mario D. Fantini agrees, listing "an understanding and appreciation of human achievement in humanities and the arts" as a major goal of education.

In *A Nation at Risk*, the NCEE said that a high school

curriculum should give students opportunities in the fine and performing arts and that these courses should demand "more rigorous effort" and require as high a level of performance as the basics.

Fine arts, music, and drama are not new to America's schools. In the early 1900s, educator John Dewey said that these courses were "not luxuries...but fundamental forces of development." And Kohl says that it is undemocratic to regard the arts as "frills and privileges...a way of saying that the pleasures provided by the arts [are for people] born into families with money to learn music, drawing, dance, filmmaking, video."

Kohl also points out that using the imagination develops the abilities needed to solve social and technical problems, as well as artistic ones: "The attempt to express feelings or ideas through art is essential for coming to terms with experience. People come to know themselves and others better through song, dance, and theater. They learn ways of organizing the visual world through painting, drawing, video, and film. All the arts provide ways of experimenting with the possible, of extending oneself and participating with others in fulfilling collective activity."

Many schools have integrated the arts with other subjects in the curriculum. In *Public Schools of Choice*, Mario Fantini describes a bilingual public school in California that includes the study of fine arts, crafts, and folklore in language classes, and a Berkeley, California, high school with a curriculum integrating "art, dance, drama, music, TV, radio, filmmaking and communication skills with an English-history-humanities core."

Art educators point out that career opportunities in commercial art, computer art, and design are expanding. "With television, ads, and magazines, everything is presented visually," says Joseph Mola, coordinator of art and music programs for the Norwalk, Connecticut, public schools.

Although Ernest Boyer and his researchers recommend that all secondary students study the arts, in *High School* they reported that in many U.S. schools the arts have been "shamefully neglected..." Yet, Boyer says, "Now, more than ever, all

A substance abuse counselor teaches a class on the physical and psychological effects of depressants.

people need to see clearly, hear acutely, and feel sensitively through the arts. These skills are ... essential if we are to survive together with civility and joy."

HEALTH EDUCATION

In order to study the arts or any other subject successfully, students must arrive at school physically and emotionally well enough to learn. Through the years, as students spent more time in schools, school involvement in health and welfare increased. Entrance to school requires immunizations against certain diseases. School nurses provide preventive and treatment services, and counselors deal with emotional and family problems.

Problems such as inadequate exercise, overweight, high levels of cholesterol, and drug and alcohol abuse among children and teenagers have led schools to develop programs that deal with many aspects of mental and physical health. Often, these programs extend from kindergarten through secondary school.

Health expert Jane E. Brody has found that health education tries "to foster physical health and safety practices, emotional health and self-esteem, and a sense of personal responsibility...[and] to educate children about how their bodies work and how habits like smoking, drugs, and alcohol can disrupt or destroy body structures and functions." Many discuss the impact of environmental health issues, too.

Recent studies show that children with three or more years of health education are less likely to abuse drugs or alcohol or to smoke cigarettes than are young people the same age who have had less than one year of health education. Their other health habits—nutrition, exercise, dental care—are also better. Teachers claim that the programs increase self-esteem and interest in learning other subjects. At a cost of about six dollars a year per student, the programs cost far less than the long-term costs of treating preventable health problems, say the experts.

Drug education courses are mandatory in some states. Newer programs, especially in the elementary grades, often focus upon enhancing self-esteem, as well as learning problem-solving skills, good judgment, techniques for withstanding peer pressure, and healthful ways to cope with stress. Students also meet in groups to discuss drug problems in their families and communities. Many people agree with Robert M. Maccarone, director of antidrug programs in Westchester County, New York, who says, "We have the audience in the schools to begin with, so why not take advantage at the earliest possible age?"

Like drug education, courses dealing with sex and AIDS are often controversial. In some states AIDS education is mandatory for all public school children, although students may be excused from attending the classes at their parents' request. Supporters of AIDS education say that teenagers are at risk. Of the more than 23,000 people in New York City who have AIDS, at least 10 percent are thought to have been infected while they were teenagers. The National Centers for Disease Control have reported that the number of AIDS cases among teens doubles every fourteen months. And students themselves are expressing more concern about AIDS: A survey published in the *Journal of Home Economics* showed that "contracting AIDS" is among the top ten worries listed by teens.

Like many similar programs, a New York City AIDS course contains scientific information and discusses drug and sexual activity, emphasizing abstinence from both. Other discussions focus upon better communication with parents, overcoming peer pressure, preventing infection, and the problems of teenage pregnancy. People have objected to these programs on religious and moral grounds, criticizing both the subject matter and the way it is presented. Some parents say that AIDS should not be discussed at school. Others say that schools can discuss AIDS but only if they teach abstinence from all sexual activity and avoid discussing "safe sex" or condoms.

One teacher says that in both AIDS and drug education, he tries to make his students look carefully at the consequences of their actions. "At this age, many kids feel they are immortal. They don't want to believe that these bad things can happen to them."

PROMOTING UNDERSTANDING AMONG ETHNIC GROUPS

Besides helping students to deal with issues regarding their personal health and well-being, some schools also discuss social issues. The problem of bigotry toward people of different races, nationalities, and religions has been addressed in different ways. Some schools use a course called "A World of Difference," initiated in Boston in 1985. Sponsored by the Anti-Defamation League of B'nai B'rith and several corporations, the program describes racism and ethnic prejudice in America, both past and present. Students discuss segregation, vandalism at churches and synagogues, violence toward minorities, and the exclusion of people from clubs and social groups. The course examines ways in which people have worked to combat prejudice.

In Pittsburgh, Pennsylvania, where public schools have almost equal numbers of black and white students, Prospect Middle School Center for Multiracial, Multicultural, and Multiethnic Education was opened in 1989. A central purpose of the school is to encourage respect and understanding among all races and to formulate model programs for other city schools.

Educators in New York, Georgia, California, and Washington, D.C., as well as other places, have examined their curricula to see if they reflect the pluralistic nature of America—the experiences, history, culture, and values of the major ethnic groups. Material about America's multicultural heritage is being added to textbooks. Educators hope that better understanding of the contributions and customs of ethnic groups will improve human relationships.

VALUES AND SCHOOLING

As schools work to combat bigotry, they are taking a position regarding certain values—respecting people whose beliefs are different from one's own, for example. People do not always agree about whether schools can—or should—formally teach values. Some people object to the content and/or teaching methods of such courses. Others worry that the time needed for academic work is lost when the schools are asked to meet so many needs. "Parents and boards of education have dumped a lot of the raising of children on the schoolteacher," says Joyce Griffin, director of the NAACP in Stamford, Connecticut. Like others, she thinks that families, religious organizations, and community groups can do more to help children.

"It seems like we are learning values in school, even when we aren't discussing them," says a twelfth-grader. "We are being taught to value learning and respect for authority. We're expected to have self-discipline, good manners, and work hard."

"Schools should not tell us how and what to think about everything," says another student. "Part of growing up is deciding how you feel and what your own values will be."

"I get my values at home and from our church," says a ninth-grader. "Mostly, I have continued to keep these same values, even though other people around me have different ones."

Teaching specific values can be a sticky issue. Problems arise when differing viewpoints clash. What one family thinks should be taught may offend certain others, especially in sensitive areas, such as religion or morals. In a very diverse society like America, it is sometimes difficult to agree on these matters.

Some educators think it is not necessary to create new courses to teach values. Diane Ravitch says that schools can promote character development "[by] recognizing that the school already has its own powerful resources, in both the formal and the implicit curriculum." Through science, she says children can learn "honesty, open-mindedness, critical thinking, and the capacity to withhold judgment in the absence of evidence." Works of literature can demonstrate "how men and women in different times and places have responded to moral dilemmas." And history "is a living laboratory in which to consider the relations among ideas, actions, and consequences."

Ravitch also emphasizes the importance of the "implicit curriculum"—or what students learn by "the life that is actually lived in the school." This includes the behavior of adults, the rules and the ways in which they are enforced, and educational policies. All offer chances to promote "responsibility, honesty, fairness, independence, kindness, courtesy, diligence, persistence, and self-discipline," Ravitch concludes.

There is typically more disagreement about the teaching of the arts, health, and values or ethics than about teaching geography or math. Health and values education touch more personal concerns and may lead to clashes between parents and schools. For these reasons, you may have a course in sex education while your cousin in another state does not. His school may offer a course in values that is unlike anything in your high school. Different states and individual schools have developed courses that they think will best suit local needs.

Because schools are often expected to deal with social problems, they are likely to continue debating what kinds of courses will promote physical, emotional, and social well-being. Students and their families can play a major role in this ongoing debate.

CHAPTER SEVEN

EARLY

INTERVENTION

AND READINESS

TO LEARN

"**WHEN** I'm twenty, I'm going to college," says Rodney, age four. Rodney lives in the Harlem section of New York City and attends Project Giant Step, a publicly funded preschool program for children from low-income families. Rodney calls his school, located in Public School 154, "excellent." The mother of another student says, "She comes home and starts doing the same things she did at school—drawing or reading. She's become much more self-directed." This parent values the attention that the preschool staff gives to each child, saying, "Schools don't always have the time to do that."

The joy that these children take in learning and the enthusiasm they feel about starting kindergarten are exactly what educators hope to achieve in a quality preschool. For children from middle- or high-income homes, such educational experiences are often possible. But many American children do not have such advantages.

In the United States one child out of every five is poor. Discussions about education reform inevitably turn to the subject of poverty, because poor children fail in school more often than children who enjoy economic advantages. They may score lower on achievement tests. They are more likely to drop out of school and less likely to pursue higher education.

Statistics from the U.S. Bureau of the Census show that children make up the largest portion of the 32 million Americans who live below the poverty line. Minority groups experience more poverty: The poverty rate for black Americans is 31.6 percent, compared to 10.1 percent for whites. For Hispanics, the rate is 26.8 percent. Forty-four percent of all black children and 38 percent of all Hispanic children are poor. These rates are expected to increase so that by the year 2000, 25 percent of all children will live in poverty.

To many experts, rising poverty means that education reforms must attempt to alleviate poverty and the problems that it can cause. Howard Howe II, commissioner of education under former President Lyndon B. Johnson, criticizes the assumption "that fixing schools will fix young people."

Howe points to the family as the main educational unit, saying that "adjusting schools to serve children who are delivered for repairs from neighborhoods and homes that have failed them is useful but not sufficient. Poor parents love their children just as much as rich parents.... But a family in poverty has a very hard time delivering a child to school with the same prospects as children from middle-class families." Howe is one of many people who worry that when children enter elementary school with so many disadvantages, they may never catch up.

READINESS FOR SCHOOL

In 1989 the Governors' Task Force discussed the issue of getting all children physically and mentally ready to start school. Governor Bill Clinton of Arkansas, a leader in the education reform movement, stated bluntly, "This country needs a comprehensive child development policy for children under five."

The Task Force was outspoken about the importance of preschool education for low-income children: "The federal government should work with states to develop and fully fund early-intervention strategies for children. All eligible children should have access to [a] preschool program with strong parental involvement." The Governors Association agreed. In February 1990 it said that every four-year-old in America should have access to a program that meets educational, social, nutritional, and health care needs.

"Head Start was always the model of what early childhood intervention should be about," asserts Edward F. Zigler, psychology professor at Yale University. Project Head Start began in 1965, a key component of President Lyndon B. Johnson's "war on poverty." It aimed to provide comprehensive services for preschool children and their families in order to alleviate problems that can stem from poverty.

As in other preschool classrooms, Head Start children learn about numbers, the alphabet, and concepts such as "large" and "small." They discuss good health habits and behavior and enjoy physical exercise, music, art activities, and games.

Parent involvement is an essential part of this program. Part of each Head Start center's budget is spent on educational workshops for parents. They can participate in the decision-making process as members of elected councils that help to direct the centers. Some parents work in Head Start programs as lunch aides, teacher aides, or parent coordinators.

The teacher tries to help the whole family feel more positive about schooling. Often, teachers make home visits. In many cases, Head Start teachers have influenced parents to get more education and to find better jobs.

Long-term studies of the Head Start program show its value: Young people who complete the program are more likely to earn a high school diploma, pursue higher education, and to be employed than children from similar backgrounds who did not

Since 1965 the Head Start program has successfully helped pre-schoolers overcome the disadvantages of poverty.

attend Head Start. They are less likely to become criminal offenders or to depend upon welfare benefits. They have lower rates of teenage pregnancy, better school attendance records, and more positive attitudes about school.

There is a debate about whether test scores in later grades accurately depict Head Start's effectiveness. These scores show that Head Start graduates do not always maintain the gains made in earlier years. Edward Zigler blames this decline on problems in the quality of schools that these children attend, as well as family and neighborhood conditions.

Rosemary Mazattenta, supervisor of Head Start in Philadelphia, contends that standardized test results are less important than the benefits of parental involvement, better health and nutrition, and more optimistic attitudes about schooling. Head Start graduates praise the ways their teachers inspired them. "My teacher told me I could be anything I want to be. She showed me I'm as good as anyone else," says a high school junior who attended Head Start in North Carolina. "I'm the first in my family to finish high school," says a recent graduate who attended the same program. "I'm going to college next fall."

In early 1990 only one of every five children eligible for Head Start was enrolled in the program. Statistics from the Department of Health and Human Services show that 450,000 children—38 percent black, 33 percent white, and 22 percent Hispanic—are now in Head Start. There was not enough funding to operate the centers needed for the other nearly two million eligible four-year-olds.

The lack of adequate funding has led to several problems. Low salaries make it difficult to recruit well-trained teachers. The centers often need repairs, as do the surrounding buildings in poor neighborhoods and housing projects. In order to serve more children, centers have to reduce the amount of money that they spend per child—for example, by enlarging class sizes.

President Bush supports Head Start: "Give any American kid an equal place at the starting line and just watch what that kid can do. Head Start helps kids get that equal place." In early 1990 the President authorized an increase in funding—$500 million per year above the $1.23 billion the program now receives. This is the largest single funding increase since Head Start began and would enable it eventually to serve about 70 percent of those eligible to join the program.

But some people want a greater increase in funding and services, so that all eligible children can enroll in a good program without delay. They would also like to have one teacher for every five children rather than one teacher for every ten children, which is a typical ratio at the centers. Educators and groups like the Children's Defense Fund also recommend that children enter such preschool programs before age four.

PARENTING PROGRAMS

Some states fund programs to help parents help their children. In 1988, Missouri set up programs in which the parents of 50,000 preschoolers attend evening classes to learn more about parenting and ways to prepare children for school. Teachers visit homes, telling parents how to enhance their children's development through reading, conversations, and family activities.

The principal at a St. Louis school said that the children whose parents attended the classes were better prepared for school: "They're more attentive. Those children just shine."

An innovative program—the Beethoven Project—was begun in 1987 in Chicago's Robert Taylor Homes, the nation's largest public housing project. There, counselors, teachers, physicians, and neighborhood paraprofessionals help pregnant women prepare for parenthood. These women, as well as mothers with babies, can receive social, medical, and educational services.

Other states and communities offer innovative family-oriented programs. In Ohio the Family Life Education program helps families in disadvantaged areas by offering classes to strengthen skills in parenting and in managing homes with limited resources. In 1989, 10,718 parents, 2,512 infants and toddlers, and 4,558 preschoolers took part in parent-child interaction courses. The staff was able to identify health problems in 820 of the children and guide the families to the proper agencies for care.

In places such as Shreveport, Louisiana, mothers who have just given birth receive hospital visits from people who share literature and information about child care.

THE NEED CONTINUES

Research points out the need to sustain progress that is made in these family education and preschool programs. Edward Zigler and others believe that as poor children continue their schooling, they need health care and social services. Unfortunately, many schools do not have enough counselors, social workers, psychologists, or nutritionists to give the kind of help that Head Start and Project Giant Step give to younger children and their families.

Although early intervention programs can accomplish a great deal, even their strongest supporters warn that this is not the only solution or a total solution for children who suffer many disadvantages. "The problems of poor people are not going to be solved by giving their children one year of preschool," Zigler says bluntly. "The problem is jobs and housing."

Still, advocates of increased funding for early childhood education point out the practical benefits: Each dollar spent by Head Start saves about six dollars in welfare, remedial education, and other costs.

As they evaluate the quality of programs for low-income children, researchers are looking at early childhood education in general. The number of American children enrolled in preschools has risen dramatically in the past twenty-five years. People are asking what kinds of programs are most beneficial.

A 1989 study sponsored by the Spencer Foundation warns about the hazards of pressuring children to learn academic subjects at very young ages. Many children, says the study, respond by showing less creativity in elementary school and by expressing more anxiety about tests. Furthermore, they do not seem to maintain the academic advantage they demonstrate at the beginning.

Does this mean that children should not learn any academics during the preschool years? Experts recommend that children be exposed to learning materials and be encouraged to explore and enjoy learning through activities. Drawing and scribbling, looking at books, listening to stories, playing games with letters and numbers—these and other activities help a child enjoy learning.

Education writer Fred M. Hechinger concludes that "the issue for poor and affluent children alike ultimately is not between pushing youngsters and just letting them play aimlessly. Research points to a middle way: letting children be children but helping them discover the joy of new knowledge and unpressured learning."

Says one preschool teacher, "Young children need to learn that effort leads to success. They must learn to feel good about themselves, to cope, to be self-reliant, and to dream."

CHAPTER EIGHT

STUDENTS

AT RISK

DISCUSSIONS about the challenges in education focused upon many different issues during the 1980s. Reports such as *A Nation at Risk* led to tighter academic standards and increases in homework and the amount of time spent on academic tasks. Later, reform advocates pointed to the need for changes throughout the system, from the bottom up, with more help for students who face special risks of school failure.

CHILDREN IN NEED

In 1985 the National Coalition of Advocates for Students released the report *Barriers to Excellence: Our Children at Risk*. The coalition stated that the most profound barrier to educational reform was "the fact that hundreds of thousands of youngsters

are not receiving even minimal educational opportunities...
many low-income students get the message that society does not
really care about their education."

The Committee for Economic Development, sponsored by
large U.S. corporations, expressed similar concerns in its 1987
report, *Children in Need: Investment Strategies for the Educationally Disadvantaged*. The committee pointed out the pitfalls of
raising academic standards for all students without giving more
help to children who might not be able to meet them, saying that
this approach could "leave a significant proportion of the
population underskilled and probably unemployable." In many
cases students were not prepared to meet already existing
standards, said the committee.

The committee recommended early childhood education,
parent involvement, and more help for students at high risk of
school failure, such as those living in poor urban or rural areas,
Native Americans, migrant farm workers' children, and the
homeless. But as the 1980s ended, experts concluded that
reforms had not succeeded in enough inner-city schools or other
schools with large numbers of low-income students.

Poverty is consistently accompanied by lower school achievement and higher dropout rates. The dropout rate, nationwide, is
close to 30 percent. The dropout rate in Los Angeles is about 39
percent; in Chicago, New York, and other cities the dropout rate
in some schools approaches or exceeds 50 percent.

Speaking about educating poor children, Albert Shanker
says, "It's true that schools could do a better job of educating
many, many more of these kids, and we must continue to raise
achievement levels. But many other systems affect the kind of
education kids get—housing, transportation, health care."

NUTRITION AND HEALTH CARE

In view of these concerns, educators have studied the problems
that afflict poor children, such as inadequate health care and
malnutrition. In 1989, the National Education Association

released a report by the Food Research and Action Center entitled "The Relationship Between Nutrition and Learning." It discussed the ways in which hunger impedes learning. Teachers described children who were faint, dizzy, tired, or experiencing hunger pains in class because they did not get breakfast or other meals at home.

"Increasingly, the face of hunger is the face of a young child," said Raymond L. Flynn, mayor of Boston, and head of the U.S. Conference of Mayors that conducted a nationwide study of hunger in 1989. The group found that in only one year, requests to various social agencies for food had risen 19 percent. Two-thirds of those seeking food were children or their parents.

Responding to the problem of hungry schoolchildren, the Save the Children Federation started a school lunch program in Harlan County, Kentucky, in 1932 during the Great Depression. This became a model for the hot-lunch programs that were later funded by the federal government. Federal funding increased during the 1960s when the Johnson administration declared "war on poverty."

About 3.7 million children benefited from school breakfast programs in 1987–88, while 12 million children received free school lunches. But more than twice as many children—26 million—got free lunches back in 1981 before budget cuts were made during the Reagan administration.

More spending cuts were proposed for the 1990 federal budget. Concerned citizens want Congress to strengthen rather than cut back school lunch programs. Mary Futrell, past president of the NEA, says that for many children, the federally funded meal they receive at school is "not only the best meal they get, it may be their only meal."

Health care is another problem for poor students. In his book *The Same Client: The Demographics of Education and Service Delivery Systems*, Harold L. Hodgkinson says that fewer U.S. children are immunized against childhood diseases than children in many other countries—50 percent fewer than in Spain or France, for instance. In addition, about one-fourth of the pregnant women in America do not receive prenatal care. This can lead to preventable health problems for their children and contributes to a national infant mortality rate that is higher than that of many other industrialized countries.

Health insurance also may be inadequate. The Campaign for Healthy Children, sponsored by the American Academy of Pediatrics, found that in New York State alone, 700,000 people under age twenty-one have no health insurance. About 600,000 others are insured, but their policies do not pay for things that children need, such as immunizations, annual check-ups, or other preventive care.

Rural poverty, with an attendant lack of health care, is a serious problem, especially in Tennessee, South Carolina, Alabama, Louisiana, Arkansas, and Mississippi. Only one-fifth of South Carolina's forty-seven counties have enough physicians.

In a *New York Times* interview, Dr. Ronald Myers, who devotes his medical practice to people living in Tchula, a Mississippi delta town, spoke for many people when he said, "Here you're putting all of this money into educational reforms and you've got these sick, malnourished kids, whose mothers never got any prenatal care. If they're not healthy, how are they going to learn?"

HOMELESS CHILDREN

Homeless children face special problems in getting an education. The lack of a home, irregular meals, noise, overcrowding, and the need for a place to study are major obstacles. The children may feel stigmatized. They fear the drugs and crime in their surroundings. Changing schools compounds these problems.

Understandably, homeless children score below the average of other public school children on standardized tests. Fewer than half read on grade level, and they are more likely than other children to fail a course or be held back a grade.

In its 1989 survey of twenty-seven cities, the U.S. Conference of Mayors noted that requests for emergency shelter had risen 25 percent since 1988. Thirty-six percent of those in shelters were families. Of America's estimated 500,000 to 750,000 homeless children, nearly half miss school regularly. A 1989 report on New York's 7,218 homeless children showed that one-third had changed schools two to six times since their families became homeless.

What is being done to help homeless children succeed in school? A provision of the Stewart McKinney Homeless Assistance Act of 1987 states that they are entitled to the same schooling as other children and to services that meet their extra needs. But funding, from state and local budgets, is often lacking.

School administrators and teachers are using different approaches. "All over the United States, scrappy educators and advocates for the homeless are teaming up to address the educational needs of the some 500,000 youngsters for whom home is a cardboard box, a welfare hotel, a car, or a concrete slab underneath an overpass," wrote Donna Harrington-Lueker, associate editor of the *Executive Educator*. In an interview for the *Educator*, Terrence Quinn, a principal in New York City, said that for some homeless children, "school is the only place that offers warmth, stability, and hope."

Mr. Quinn and other principals hold programs after school and give children needed school supplies and alarm clocks. Like other educators, these principals think that tutoring, meals, bus services, and counseling are vital. They also think that children should be allowed to do their homework on school premises.

In Boston and several other cities, homeless children can continue to attend the same school, even if their family moves to a different shelter. Some New York teachers also go to welfare hotels to teach. This reduces the disruption caused by changes in schools, teachers, and classmates.

At the Coeur d'Alene Elementary School in Venice, California, 20 to 30 percent of the children are homeless. Lesson plans are often interrupted as children come and go. Because their schooling is erratic, many children have what principal Beth Ojena describes as "great gaps in their learning"—for example, third-graders may not know the alphabet. To help these children, the school serves both breakfast and lunch and provides a place for them to take naps. The staff includes a nurse, counselor, psychologist, and teaching assistant. Studies show that programs like these make a difference. In schools with support services for children and families, the academic achievement of homeless children rises significantly.

MIGRANT FARM WORKERS

Like homeless children, children of migrant farm workers face problems in school. More than half drop out before the ninth grade, and only 11 to 12 percent enter the twelfth grade, according to the U.S. Department of Health and Human Services.

The obstacles that migrant workers face include health problems, frequent changes of schools, isolation (due to language barriers and embarrassment about the family's occupation), and school absences caused by working in the fields or traveling from job to job.

Many migrant workers value education. They enroll their children in school, wherever the family goes to work. Hundreds of migrant children attend Head Start programs, and hundreds more are on waiting lists. Migrant workers also use the services provided by a federally funded program called the Migrant Education Fund. The fund provides a dropout-prevention program, tutoring, and literacy classes in English, and also seeks to involve parents in their children's education.

A program called Yo Puedo—"I Can"—is based in Santa Cruz, California, in an area where more than ten thousand migrant children live. High school–age students attend a summer program at the local University of California campus. They go to classes from 8:00 A.M. to 5:30 P.M. and study again with teachers during evening sessions. The classes combine academics with skills in problem-solving, leadership, communication, and cultural enrichment to enhance ethnic pride.

The program, funded by the county and federal governments, has been highly praised. Many Yo Puedo graduates enter colleges, Princeton University and Cornell University among them. One parent said that the program "motivates the parents as well as the students." Participant Eugenia Ortiz says, "It builds confidence and gives us the motivation to continue our education."

CHILD LABOR

Migrant workers are not the only children whose work may interfere with their schooling. Although the Federal Fair Labor Standards Act, passed in 1936, prohibits children younger than age sixteen from working in factories, violations are common and seem to be increasing.

In 1990 inspectors in New York City found young children working in garment-district factories and in restaurants and supermarkets. Many of the children were recent immigrants or poor children whose families needed income. Some employers admitted they broke the laws because of the labor shortage or because parents brought their children to work.

In response, the Labor Department conducted a special investigation and has increased its efforts to find and penalize employers who break the law. Congress also plans to enact stiffer penalties for these crimes.

Child-advocacy groups agree that these children miss too much school. If they do attend, they are too tired to do their best. Hugh McDaid, director of the Apparel Industry Task Force, said, "It is a trap for them. They sacrifice their education and literally commit themselves to a life working in a sweatshop."

NATIVE AMERICANS

During the 1980s, little progress was made in raising the school achievement levels of Native American students. As a group, Native Americans (Alaska natives and American Indians) have a dropout rate twice as high as that of other U.S. students. Fewer than 10 percent receive college degrees.

Native Americans have faced some unique problems in our society. Their ancestors were displaced from tribal lands, then assigned to government-designated areas called reservations. Many white settlers considered the customs and religions of Native Americans to be inferior and tried to persuade, even to force, Native Americans to change their ways and convert to Christianity. Government policies aimed to suppress the various Indian cultures.

In 1967, a special Senate committee was appointed to study American Indian education. After spending two years visiting schools and holding hearings around the United States, the committee announced, "We are shocked at what we discovered. ...Our national policies for educating American Indians are a failure of major proportions. They have not offered Indian children—either in years past or today—an educational opportunity anywhere near equal to that offered the great bulk of American children."

The committee stressed the importance of a curriculum that reflects Indian culture and said that more bilingual programs were needed. It recommended that Native Americans have more control in planning and administering their own schools and in working with public school officials to meet their special needs.

Funding for Native American programs comes from the Bureau of Indian Affairs and the U.S. Department of Education. Since 1981 funding has decreased by about 27 percent when inflation is considered. Yet Native Americans suffer from unemployment, health problems, shorter life expectancies than other Americans, malnutrition, and other effects of poverty.

Considering these obstacles and the lack of funding, can progress be made during the coming decades?

Education Secretary Lauro F. Cavazos acknowledges that, for years, educational programs for Native Americans have been marred by "crossed purposes and unfulfilled hopes." In 1989 he asked a group of educators, including Native Americans, to study these problems.

DROPOUTS: A CLOSER LOOK

Sixteen-year-old Juan C. recalls that a few years ago, he planned to drop out of school. "Sometimes I would think, 'I must be the dumbest kid in the school.' I couldn't even tell time. I would look at the clock and panic and get angry about it. I'd say, 'Forget this' and just walk out of the classroom." What made a difference for Juan was a caring teacher who offered extra help and kept saying, "I know you have it in you."

Many young people make the opposite choice—they leave school before graduating. Reducing the dropout rate is a major national goal for the year 2000.

A 1983 report by the Department of Education listed reasons that students themselves give for dropping out of school. These reasons include pregnancy, poor grades, the desire to work full-time, a feeling that "school wasn't for me," and "not getting along with teachers." Some students gave more than one reason.

Researchers from Columbia University Teachers College in New York City have identified these factors among school dropouts: poverty, a single-parent home, and a mother who is herself a high school dropout or who speaks a primary language other than English. Black and Hispanic children are at higher risk. Experts conclude that this is because more black and Hispanic children live in poverty with a single parent.

Students who drop out often have a history of poor school attendance and they are older than average for their grade level. Another indication of risk is the failure to acquire basic academic skills, like reading, before entering high school.

In analyzing why kids drop out, there has been a shift from trying to figure out what's wrong with the dropouts to focusing on what might be wrong with the schools themselves. Such an approach has led many schools to change their structure and their courses.

Jeanne Frankl, executive director of the Public Education Association, a citizens' group, says that high schools and middle schools can be "large, anonymous, and boring. Except for a few school districts where there has been some innovation, the program, structure, and climate of these schools is very off-putting to young adolescents."

A twelve-year-old student describes the transition to middle school: "Suddenly, there was all this homework and the courses were much harder. We had to change classes, and I was in different classes from my friends. I could have used more help."

Programs have been developed to address these problems. Some middle and high schools offer smaller classes, after-school and summer sessions, tutoring, and counseling for students and families. They hope this will ease the transition from the smaller, more familiar setting of the elementary school, where at least one teacher gets to know a child well, to the larger, more anonymous secondary schools.

In 1987 the Office of Educational Research and Improvement published *Dealing with Dropouts: The Urban Superintendents' Call to Action*. The administrators, who had experience working in schools throughout the United States, offered six major strategies for improving achievement and preventing dropout:

1. Intervene early, with preschool programs and close monitoring of progress in early grades before feelings of academic failure damage self-esteem or reduce the pleasure of learning.

2. Develop a positive school climate, one with "strong leaders who stress academic achievement, maintain an orderly and disciplined environment, and work with staff to instill positive values and self-confidence in students."

3. Set high expectations for attendance, academics, and behavior. Make rules clear and enforce them consistently.

4. Select and develop strong teachers "who are sensitive to the needs of at-risk students."

5. Provide a broad range of instructional programs for students with widely different needs, such as pregnant teenagers and those who miss school frequently. The group suggests magnet schools and alternative schools that offer special curricula or smaller classes.

   Also recommended are comprehensive programs for children who do not speak English. Some programs, as in Seattle, Washington, are bilingual, usually for Spanish-speaking children. They combine instruction with counseling and Hispanic history and culture.

6. Encourage collaborative efforts among schools, communities, churches, and families, with "jointly planned and administered programs."

As the 1990s began, many schools were starting programs that reflect these six guidelines. They were also trying to cope with other problems—teenage pregnancy, substance abuse, and disruption and violence in the nation's schools.

TEENAGE PREGNANCY

Every weekday, Ruth C., age seventeen, rises at 6:00 A.M. in order to get ready for school. She needs extra time to dress and feed her eighteen-month-old son and to pack the bag he will need at the day-care center operated by Ruth's high school. She hurries to the center, then gets to her own classes by 8:00 A.M. Evenings, her mother watches the baby while Ruth works at a local grocery store.

Ruth is one of the nation's half-million teenage mothers. The teen pregnancy rate is estimated at one million per year, which

In many schools, special classes allow pregnant teenagers to continue their academic courses and to learn about child care.

means that one out of every ten girls aged fifteen to nineteen becomes pregnant annually. The number of adolescent mothers who are unmarried (70 percent) has more than doubled since the 1970s when the rate was 30 percent.

These statistics have serious consequences for the education of both the mothers and their children. Both face high risks of school dropout and unemployment.

As of 1989 fourteen of the fifty states were funding infant and child care for adolescent mothers attending school. Such services can be expensive, and some critics complain that by providing day care for unmarried mothers, schools give teenagers the message that premarital sexual activity is acceptable.

But those who advocate such programs—while still urging teenagers to avoid pregnancy—believe that it is important to help the mothers finish high school, if only to avoid welfare costs to taxpayers. "Teen-mother programs are probably the most cost-effective programs we have," says Grace Hibma, consultant to the Los Angeles County school system, which offers child-care programs.

Ohio started a program called GRADS (Graduation, Reality, and Dual-Role Skills) to keep teenage mothers in school. In 1985 the dropout rate for students in the program was 16 percent, rather than the 80 percent rate nationwide. The program provides low-cost day care, counseling services, and group discussions for the mothers, who attend regular classes with other students. Programs like GRADS have been started in other states. Directors of these programs say that without social services and counseling, day-care services are not enough.

DRUGS AND THE SCHOOLS

"Our biggest problem." That was the conclusion reached by high school teachers in a 1989 survey conducted by Phi Delta Kappa, the fraternal society for teachers.

Students who use drugs face many risks. Where families or communities are abusing drugs, it hurts students, even when they avoid drugs themselves. "If those children come into my classroom and they have been up all night because someone in the house is using drugs, that impacts on what I teach," said Mary Futrell, former president of the National Education Association.

In many neighborhoods children must pass drug dealers in the streets when they walk to and from school. Street gangs pressure them to use and sell drugs. Investigating this problem, journalist Dirk Johnson found that when school ends, "some students volunteer to do chores for teachers...biding time, waiting for the drug dealers and gang members to leave the sidewalks so they can dash home—a bit more safely."

Johnson met a fourteen-year-old boy whose friends became gang members, then rejected him because he refused to use drugs. This boy sees other teenagers earn $100 to $200 a week selling drugs. "I stay in this house all the time," he said. "If you go outside, people will jump you....I get real tempted to join a gang and sell drugs. Then I wouldn't have to worry about getting beaten up."

While the government tries different approaches, schools are grappling with the problem through education programs, stricter rules, undercover police officers, and the enforcement of dress and hair codes that forbid styles associated with the "drug cultures." Some schools use drug and Breathalyzer (for alcohol) testing. In one Florida school with a strong drug education program, students caught using drugs must attend a rehabilitation program. In Las Vegas, parents must accompany the students to rehabilitation programs. Other schools urge students to report any illicit drug use that they observe in school.

In some drug-plagued neighborhoods, groups of neighbors have organized escort services to accompany children to and from school. Communities have also established "drug-free" zones where children can play safely while neighborhood volunteers patrol the area to keep criminals out.

Teenagers are concerned about the abuse of drugs, including alcohol.Some concerned teens have joined groups like SADD (Students Against Drunk Drivers), which try to educate people about the dangers of alcohol abuse and urge people not to drink if they plan to drive a motor vehicle. Concerned parents cooperate with such efforts by pledging to maintain "safe homes"—homes in which alcoholic beverages are not served to teens.

Reducing alcohol and drug use among young people is one of the most critical challenges facing the nation. An eighth-grader from New Jersey who has decided never to use drugs offers this advice: "Don't get into drugs, you're only hurting yourself and the people who care about you."

MAKING SCHOOLS SAFE

In public opinion polls, Americans express concern that there is not enough discipline in the schools and that today's students do not respect authority. Teachers report more disruptive incidents than they reported ten or twenty years ago.

The National Institute of Education has revealed disturbing statistics about school crime in America. During every month of 1989, more than 5,000 secondary teachers and almost 300,000 students were physically attacked at school. These assaults included hitting, pushing someone against a wall, even rape, stabbing, and shooting.

Teachers and administrators have found students bringing handguns and knives into schools. In 1988 a seventeen-year-old student was shot and killed a few blocks from his Washington, D.C., school. In Texas a fourteen-year-old boy with a .38 pistol held an assistant principal hostage for two hours. A fifteen-year-old Chicago student was shot and killed by a classmate whom he had accused of hitting his girlfriend. Students express fear of being attacked by other students who want their money or possessions—clothing, shoes, rings, or gold chains.

Law-enforcement officers claim that much of the violence is related to drugs, especially crack cocaine. Profits enable teen-agers to buy guns, which may be sold on the street for only twenty-five dollars. Violence in the schools is also blamed on the violence that young people see around them, on urban streets as well as on television and at the movies.

The National Education Association has formed state task forces to study violence in the schools. The NEA believes that each state must provide safe schools for the sake of all concerned and that programs should include both prevention and security.

Many schools cope with this problem by hiring security guards. Building doors are locked after employees and students are inside. Dogs sniff for drugs. Metal detectors have been installed in some schools to prevent students from bringing weapons inside. Detroit and New York are among the cities using metal detectors in schools.

Speaking about the issue of school safety, an Atlanta high school teacher, Carolyn Hart, called school security basic:

"People can't function properly when they fear for their well-being."

ARE THE GOALS ATTAINABLE?

Safe, drug-free schools; a dropout rate that is reduced to 10 percent by the year 2000—these are substantial challenges for America's schools and for the nation as a whole.

As of 1990 only one state—Minnesota—graduated more than 90 percent of its high school students. How can the rest of the nation hope to reach that level within the next decade?

A recent program in New York City raises serious questions about one way to prevent students from dropping out. From 1985 through 1989, the city school system tested new programs costing about $8,000 per student. Students received more counseling and visits from neighborhood workers. Their parents were notified about problems and nonattendance. Yet fewer than half of the students improved their attendance or passed more courses.

Many educators claim that these results show the need for intervention earlier than high school and a need to focus on the reasons that students decide to leave school. Students who return to school and find the same kinds of classes and structure will probably leave again, say these critics: Fix the schools so students will want to stay.

A Los Angeles student who had planned to drop out before he attended a special program at Odyssey High School described his "comeback" in a graduation speech. At his former school, he said, "I felt I was nobody. They would just look at me and say, 'This guy is going to be a bum.' The day finally came when they transferred me to Odyssey....I was thinking of just dropping out of school....Odyssey is not just a high school; it's a family. A family loves and cares for one another, and that's what Odyssey does. Everyone at Odyssey helped me a lot. They never gave up on me; they stood behind me all the way."

Many young people agree that a special teacher or a school staff that cares about them and gives them individual support has influenced them to stay in school. Other students stay because they hope to get a good job or pursue higher education or because they like the school and the courses and the activities it offers. Efforts to reduce the dropout rate address all these things—teaching and administration, school structure, and ways to link schools with jobs or with higher education.

CHAPTER NINE

TEACHING:

CORNERSTONE

OF EDUCATION

"**THIS** year I considered changing jobs again," says a second-grade teacher who has spent twelve years in the classroom. "Why do I continue teaching? There is a tremendous challenge and satisfaction that comes from helping young people to learn and grow. I think teaching is one of the few professions in which you can truly change lives and make a contribution to society."

In *The Troubled Crusade* author Diane Ravitch discusses the 1945 Senate hearings, held to consider giving federal aid to schools. The Committee on Education and Labor met with teachers struggling to meet the needs of children in impoverished districts. A Mississippi teacher told the committee about the factory job she held every summer to augment her $600 salary. A teacher from rural Nebraska said that she could earn more money in a bomber plant. "But I would rather stay in the teaching profession. Somebody has got to teach those children, and I would like to do it."

There have always been people who would rather teach—despite inadequate salaries, crowded classrooms, lack of supplies, and other problems. A teacher's concern about students often goes beyond the classroom. During the Great Depression, teachers gave food and clothing to needy students. During one month in 1932, New York City teachers raised $260,000 for children. In Chicago and other cities, teachers worked during the Depression even after their paychecks stopped. Presumably, they, too, felt they "would rather teach."

TEACHERS AND EDUCATION REFORM

One of the first things any student mentions in regard to school is, of course, teachers. Teachers and the teaching process are frequently discussed in reports about education; quality teaching underlies the national education goals for the year 2000.

In 1986 the Carnegie Task Force on Teaching as a Profession issued *"A Nation Prepared: Teachers for the 21st Century."* This report said that teachers need better training, so that they can "assume new powers and responsibilities to redesign schools for the future."

People who favor giving teachers more control over school policies say that this would improve student performance and heighten teacher motivation. Others think that teachers should not be policy- or decision-makers. That role, they say, belongs to school administrators and local school boards. School systems around the nation are debating the role of teachers as they try out new ways of making decisions in the schools.

Reports on education focus on important issues about teaching. Researchers say that the United States will need a million more teachers during the 1990s. Another concern is how to define standards for teachers and how to evaluate their performance. Teacher salaries and status must be improved, say many people, and teachers need more opportunities for continuing education in order to master new skills.

In *A Nation at Risk* the NCEE said that not enough well-qualified people are joining the teaching profession, and that "many teachers are being drawn from the bottom quarter of graduating high school and college students." The NCEE contended that some teachers do not take enough courses in the subjects that they will later teach. The commission identified a major shortage of teachers for certain disciplines, including mathematics, science, and foreign languages. Other studies point to regional shortages of teachers, especially in inner cities.

DEALING WITH THE TEACHER SHORTAGE

What can be done to increase the number of teachers? Some states, such as New Jersey, have developed alternative licensing programs so that people without education degrees can teach. People who have at least a bachelor's degree and expertise in a subject can start teaching after they pass a teacher examination. By completing education classes, often at night, they can gain certification. In early 1990 twenty-three states had such programs.

Critics of alternative certification, including some teachers' unions, say that knowledge of subject matter alone does not lead to quality teaching. Teachers should understand theories of teaching and learning, among other things, say these people.

While alternative certification increases the number of teachers, other programs draw them to the areas where they are most needed. When Wendy Kopp was a senior at Princeton University, she attended a conference about education, and it gave her an idea: Why not develop a program like the Peace Corps for teachers? Ms. Kopp's "Teach for America" program recruits recent college graduates into teaching, especially to

A student teacher reads to a first-grader in Washington, D.C. In the 1990s, considerable efforts are being made to recruit talented college students for teaching careers.

inner-city schools. By teaching for two years, participants can postpone repaying their federal college loans. Trainees attend summer sessions to learn teaching techniques and to become acquainted with the culture in which they will be working. Los Angeles, New York, Washington, D.C., rural Texas, and Chicago are part of this program.

In New York City, a Peace Corps Fellows Program is working with the Board of Education to send former Peace Corps volunteers to schools in Harlem and the South Bronx. The U.S. Congress is considering a new version of the federally financed Teacher Corps, which began during the 1960s. By committing themselves to teach for five years in low-income urban or rural areas, participants would get salaries as well as money for their own further education.

Finding enough minority teachers continues to be a problem. In some cities with many black, Hispanic, or Asian-American students, there are few teachers from these groups. A *New York*

Times editorial said that attracting well-qualified minority teachers will "require aggressive recruitment, more internships, incentives like tuition reimbursement and alternative-certification programs for mid-career professionals."

In addition to the shortage of new people entering the teaching profession, there are many teachers who leave their jobs each year. Low-income urban schools have an especially high turnover, as do other schools where crowded classrooms, rundown facilities, inadequate auxiliary staff, and students with many needs place extra burdens upon teachers.

One teacher, called an outstanding educator by her peers and students, often considers changing jobs. She says, "I don't have the freedom or resources I need to teach all of my students effectively.... the bureaucratic system here is incredibly slow." Other teachers point to a lack of recognition, few opportunities to increase their knowledge and skills, and insufficient salaries. Some are frustrated by the apathy of students and parents.

Many teachers say that their schools need more money. Says a New York City teacher, "Our school was built in 1913. Overcrowding is not a problem, but the condition of the school certainly is. Classroom walls are a patchwork of fresh paint and crumbling plaster. We have no custodian, so the floors are rarely swept. Classes are expected to share textbooks and supplies."

For these and other reasons—problems such as crime and violence in schools, drug and alcohol abuse, and a lack of support from parents and the community—some teachers decide to change professions.

ARE CONDITIONS IMPROVING?

In 1989, Louis Harris and Associates surveyed two thousand teachers in grades K–12 nationwide and found that teacher morale had improved since the early 1980s. More than half of the teachers felt that they were respected as professionals; 92 percent thought that the quality of education in their schools was high.

What about salaries? A 1989 report by the American Federation of Teachers said that salaries were higher than ever before. In the 1988–89 school year, the average salary for teachers in the fifty states was $29,629. But Albert Shanker, AFT president, says that when inflation is taken into account, salaries have risen only "approximately forty-one dollars per year" since 1972.

The AFT survey found wide variations in pay among the fifty states. Alaska had the highest average salary ($41,832), while South Dakota had the lowest ($20,525). The AFT concluded that when cost of living is considered, the states with the highest salaries are Alaska, California, Michigan, Minnesota, New York, and Wisconsin.

Do teachers think needed reforms are taking place? Jane Usdan, AFT spokesperson says, "Parts of the reform movement are really happening, but they aren't happening everywhere. There are places where you have an enlightened superintendent or a school board willing to take chances, but if none of those things come together, you don't really have reform."

EDUCATING TEACHERS

The ways that teachers themselves are educated have been studied and criticized. Most teachers graduate from college with a degree in education, rather than in the subject area they will teach. Critics say that some education courses are not as challenging or important as a thorough knowledge of subject matter. Yet many teachers say that their education courses taught them how students learn and gave them valuable teaching skills. Educators are looking for the best combination of education theory and subject matter courses.

In *High School*, Ernest Boyer offers his plan for educating teachers: All would complete a core of common courses and a major in an academic discipline. During a fifth year, teachers would observe classrooms and gain teaching experience. Boyer says that all teachers should study these four areas: history of education and current issues regarding schooling in America;

learning theory and research; writing, both as an essential language tool and as a means of teaching critical thinking skills; and the use of technology and new teaching tools.

As for continuing education, many teachers complain that such programs are weak or not available. Teachers say that too many workshops are just lectures given by "experts" with no practical teaching experience.

Yet teachers and others think that ongoing education is essential. They want more summer conferences, fellowships, and opportunities to watch talented colleagues at work. Often, teachers initiate programs in order to learn about new teaching techniques, computers, cooperative learning, or ways to enhance student skills, such as critical thinking.

STANDARDS OF QUALITY TEACHING

Standards for teachers and methods of evaluating their skills are the subject of much debate. In 1986, Connecticut adopted the Education Enhancement Act, which increased teacher salaries and raised teaching standards. A section of the act called BEST—Beginning Educators' Support and Training Program—requires teachers to demonstrate competence during their first year of teaching in order to keep their state certification.

In planning this system, the Department of Education worked to define effective teaching—"what every teacher must know and be able to do," according to Commissioner Gerald N. Tirozzi. Educational research, along with input from hundreds of educators throughout the state, was used to develop guidelines for assessing teachers. Teachers are judged upon their "ability to promote a positive learning environment, maintain appropriate standards of behavior, present appropriate lesson content, develop a lesson to promote achievement of objectives, communicate clearly, and monitor student understanding."

When discussing teachers, students often mention these same

qualities, sometimes using different words. One eighth-grader says, "I like when the teacher is friendly but still can get respect from the class. If kids don't respect a teacher, they take advantage. It wastes the class time, yelling at the same kids over and over."

A tenth-grader thinks that communication is important: "When a teacher goes too fast, especially in math or science, I can get lost. Sometimes they don't let you ask questions. You feel too stupid to keep asking."

Says a twelfth-grader, "I never thought much about whether teachers had a 'goal' for each class period. But I had this teacher last year that told us at the start of each class what we were going to learn and why. It helped me pay attention, and I learned more."

TEACHER EVALUATION

How do formal teacher-evaluation programs work? In Connecticut teams of assessors (teachers, administrators, and Department of Education staff or professors trained in the program) visit the classroom six times during the year and give feedback to the teacher. Officials hope that this strong assessment program and higher salaries will increase teacher prestige and promote higher-quality teaching throughout the state.

In order to renew their certificates, many states require teachers to continue studying. In Connecticut, they must complete ninety hours of professional development courses every five years. The courses cover classroom management, new teaching techniques, language arts skills, science, mathematics, and communication skills, among other subjects.

Critics of teacher-assessment programs worry that states will impose too many regulations or even politicize the evaluation process. They also wonder whether teaching can be measured according to a fixed set of rules; a "cookbook formula" may result in "a cookie-cutter approach to teacher education," according to Lawrence D. Klein, education professor at Central Connecticut State University.

NATIONAL CERTIFICATION

A national system of certification for teachers is proposed for the 1990s. In 1987 the Carnegie Forum on Education and the Economy founded the National Board for Professional Teaching Standards. The board will develop a national certification program for experienced primary and secondary school teachers who meet rigid standards. Certification will be voluntary, but the board has predicted that at least half of the nation's 2.5 million teachers will try for certification. It will supplement but not replace teacher certification by individual states.

In its report, the board members, most of whom are teachers, say that certification will focus on how effectively a teacher helps students to learn. The board also expects that teachers will make more decisions about what and how to teach.

The voluntary certification program will begin in 1993 and aims to increase the status of the teaching profession, identify the most capable teachers, improve salaries, and thus encourage more qualified and talented people to become teachers.

TEACHERS SPEAK

What makes a good teacher? What are the problems and rewards of the profession? What should be done to improve schools? Teachers have plenty to say about these and other issues.

Jelena Morrison, who teaches high school math in Maywood, Illinois, says that "to be a good teacher, you have to go in your students' door and take them out yours." And Jacquelyn Sweetner Caffey, who teaches remedial reading at an inner-city school in Detroit, emphasizes building student self-esteem along

Inner-city educator Marva Collins says the formula for good teaching is "values and morality and good literature and getting children to love you and look up to you."

with academics. Her students make lists of things they used to think they couldn't do, then hold funerals to "bury the lists." Both of these talented teachers were featured in a documentary, "The Truth About Teachers," broadcast in September 1989.

Why do teachers teach? Mary Futrell, former president of the NEA, said that for thousands of teachers, the welfare of students is the "number-one concern.... After all, the reason we became teachers was to help students learn and to prepare them for the challenges of the future."

After nearly forty years on the job, an Ohio teacher says, "I work with young people who have been knocked down and who are not really sure why they are in school. My students deserve what every other student deserves—to have someone care about them and their future. It's my job and the job of every teacher to motivate all students. No exceptions. Period."

An English teacher in a suburban New England middle

school says, "The rewards of my work have been many.... I'll never forget those countless kids that made me laugh every day, and those parents who've been incredibly wonderful, friendly, and supportive.... With such gratifying rewards that often come months or even years after my initial contact with students, I gladly teach, and so I choose to remain a teacher."

STUDENTS SPEAK

What do students want from teachers? Many of them appreciate individual attention. "I like when a teacher gets to know me and finds out what I think," says an eighth-grader at a large urban middle school. A classmate adds, "Teachers can be nice but still show that they are in charge. My favorite teachers are the ones who know a lot and also have a good sense of humor."

Other students count on a teacher to make school interesting. "The best teachers I had didn't teach straight from the book," says a recent graduate. "They brought things to class and used books and articles besides the textbook to make the course interesting." A seventh-grader says, "When a teacher just stands there and talks, my mind wanders.... I just about fall asleep." "I know I should motivate myself," says a high school senior. "But sometimes I need the teachers to get me started."

Knowledge. Individualized attention. Interesting lessons that help to motivate students. Friendly but still able to maintain discipline. Students and others in the community expect a great deal from teachers. And all agree that quality teaching is essential for good schools.

CHAPTER TEN

SCHOOL REFORM:

CHANGING STRUCTURES,

CHANGING CHOICES

IN March 1990 the Kentucky General Assembly made a radical change in the way the state's fifteen hundred public schools are managed and funded: It voted to decentralize schools, giving local districts more power over daily operations, including curriculum and textbooks. Starting in 1991 schools would be judged by how well their students perform. Schools and teachers that succeed will be rewarded. Those that do not will have to improve, with state help—or risk being shut down.

Kentucky is not the first state to enact reforms in order to improve education. The state began planning these reforms after a 1989 state supreme court ruling that Kentucky's system of funding school districts was unconstitutional. There was a large variation in the amounts spent per pupil in different districts, ranging from $1,800 to $4,200. In addition, Kentucky students have been scoring lower on standardized academic tests than students in most other states. Under the new system schools will be evaluated for their success in reducing dropout rates and improving the health of students, among other things.

Critical reports about U.S. schools prompted many reforms during the 1980s. Changes included revising curricula and teaching methods, allowing parents and students to shop for schools, offering new programs and services, and changing the structure and decision-making processes of schools.

SCHOOL FUNDING METHODS

Several states have changed their financing systems after concerned citizens challenged spending patterns that had led to gaps between rich and poor districts. Historically, local real estate taxes have provided money for public education. Thus school districts rich in property can collect enough taxes to finance generous school budgets. Poor districts with much lower tax bases have difficulty funding their schools.

Poorer schools also have more trouble attracting and retaining highly qualified teachers, say their administrators. The school superintendent in East Orange, New Jersey, says that about 10 percent of the teachers in his district leave each year. He would like funds to add more psychologists, social workers, and counselors to help students cope with poverty, emotional problems resulting from drug and alcohol abuse, and the child abuse that some of them endure at home.

Since the 1970s, many states have tried to equalize school funding by paying a greater share of education costs, especially in those districts with the greatest need. Some states now pay for half of the educational costs within their borders.

Texas is among the states that have decided to equalize school funding. In 1989 the Texas supreme court noted "glaring disparities" between rich and poor districts after a lawsuit was filed by sixty-eight Texas school districts with low tax bases. The court opinion declared that the state legislature "must develop a plan to educate its populace efficiently and provide for a general diffusion of knowledge statewide."

In Kentucky the state supreme court devised a system of funding which lets wealthier districts exceed an "equalized rate" of spending by 30 percent. For example, if the state determines that $3,000 will be spent per year for every pupil, wealthier districts could supplement this amount and spend up to $3,900—30 percent more than $3,000.

Dr. Frank Newman, president of the Education Commission of the States, says that these rulings raise important issues: "Wealthy districts say, 'We can do more. Why should our kids be denied?'... The Constitutional issue is: Can you hold back the wealthy district?" How will states pay for these changes? Some experts predict that states will impose new taxes or increase taxes that already exist.

CHOICE IN PUBLIC SCHOOLS

The idea of "consumer choice" in regard to schools has gained increasing attention since the 1960s. Many people agree with the urban superintendents' position in the report *Dealing with Dropouts* that families should pick a school that suits the students' abilities, needs, and interests. The superintendents think such a choice is even more important for students at risk of dropping out, and say, "Some youngsters learn best in a highly structured environment. Others flourish in a freer atmosphere. A promising pianist may favor a performing arts school. A teenager who likes to tinker with cars may prefer a school that provides training in auto mechanics."

Magnet schools are an innovative way to permit choice and to achieve voluntary integration in schools. These schools specialize in subjects like math, science, or performing arts. Students who live in a city or region can apply for enrollment. According to *Dealing with Dropouts*, magnet schools have "higher attendance and lower dropout rates than the average district."

In New Rochelle, New York, the Daniel Webster Magnet School is widely praised, with more applicants than it has room for. It has achieved a racial balance in a mostly black neighborhood. One of 225 magnet schools in the state, Webster serves 420 black, white, Hispanic, and Asian students. They earn the highest scores on standardized math, writing, and reading tests of any elementary students in the city.

Magnet schools may cost more than other schools. To fund its extra programs in art, languages, and humanities, Webster School received $1.2 million, about 66 percent of its budget, from the state in 1989–90. In Dallas, magnet schools spend about twice as much per student as the other public schools in the city. Magnet schools are funded by state or local budgets, as well as by federal monies or philanthropic organizations.

"Alternative schools" are designed to help students who did not progress in traditional school environments. Students who attend these schools may have been failing courses or been disruptive or hostile. A number of alternative schools provide remedial education and vocational training. Others work with teenagers who have chronic behavior problems, including criminal behavior. Such schools usually stress parental involvement and family counseling and put families in touch with community services. Some alternative schools work only with former dropouts. Individual attention and smaller classes may enable the schools to serve students more effectively.

There is an ongoing debate about whether to give parents education vouchers—certificates worth a certain amount of money to pay for education in any private, parochial, or public school of their choice. Education vouchers or tax credits would make schools competitive, say supporters of this idea. In a related plan, families would be able to choose from among various public schools. Supporters claim that parents and children should be able to choose any school in their city or district—or even the state. Some states, including Arkansas, Iowa, Minnesota, and Nebraska, have statewide open enrollment.

People who believe families should choose their schools think that it makes schools more accountable for their performance. They believe that such a "free market" education system would improve the quality of education and increase the diversity of programs because schools would have to compete with each other to attract students. Such a system also empowers parents who cannot afford to buy homes in wealthier school districts.

How do programs of public school choice work in practice? In East Harlem, New York City, people can choose from among fifty-two public schools located in twenty buildings. Before this program began in the 1970s, math and reading scores for students in East Harlem were last (thirty-second) in the city. Test scores have improved—students now rank sixteenth—and attendance is higher. Disruptive incidents have also decreased.

What if too many students want to attend the same school? States have various plans to handle this problem, such as first-come, first-enrolled systems; lotteries; giving priority to a current student's siblings; or conducting entrance exams.

A federally funded experimental program of school choice was conducted in the Alum Rock Unified School District near San Jose, California, between 1972 and 1976. Fourteen of the twenty-four elementary and middle schools participated, developing fifty-five "minischools" with different kinds of curricula. One teacher who took part said that she had welcomed the chance to try out creative new programs, but that the competition among minischools had led to divisiveness among teachers. But superintendent William J. Jeffords claimed that the experiment made staff members more responsive to student needs.

This study concluded that location plays a key role in the choice of a school: Eighty percent of the parents said that it had been the major factor in their choice. Also, the study said that middle-class parents and those with a higher education level had obtained more comprehensive information about the schools while making their decisions. R. Gary Bridge, associate professor of psychology and education at Columbia University Teachers College, says that this finding raises questions about the ability of low-income parents with less education to make well-informed educational choices or give their children "the same kind of educational support from the home that middle-class kids get."

The National Educational Association has expressed some reservations about plans that let students attend any school they choose. NEA president Keith Geiger is among the many people who say that the best solution is to raise the level of excellence in every school and to develop more magnet and alternative public schools. Some educators call school choice a political ploy; still others fear that there is not enough room for students in the "best" schools, or that choice plans might lead to segregation of children by race, income, or ethnic group.

A report by the Educational Visions Team of the New World Foundation in New York City says that such plans must be carefully designed in order to "equalize resources, mandate open admissions and retention, expand guidance services for parents and students, and simultaneously upgrade the quality of comprehensive schools."

Ann Bastian of the New World Foundation urges people to examine choice plans closely to see how well they suit community needs and whether they "serve quality, equality, and diversity in schooling." Says Bastian, "Our assessment must recognize what choice cannot accomplish. Choice is no substitute for adequate funding or qualified teaching." Nonetheless, there is support for the development of choice systems. As Fred M. Hechinger says, "Without competition, systems cling to the status quo, even when all indicators demand change."

Students and parents have different opinions about choosing a school. "All the schools in our town are very similar," says a tenth-grader living in a community of 23,000 people. "I'm not sure it would make a difference. But maybe they would start some new things if the schools were competing for students."

"I would like to go to a nicer school," says a seventh-grader attending an inner-city school. "Some of the schools in towns outside the city have computers and other things we don't have.

They have smaller classes. We don't have a library or some things like that here, and all the rooms are crowded."

"I like this school a lot," says a fourteen-year-old who chose an arts-oriented school in East Harlem. "I love the performing classes, but also math—we have a super math program here."

"I would hate to go to a school outside my neighborhood," says a thirteen-year-old. "I like being in school with the kids I play with outside of school."

A parent expresses some common concerns: "I need to be close enough to the school to attend meetings and pick up my child in an emergency. I'm also concerned that schools teach every child the basics, no matter what other special programs they offer. I would worry if my child chose to study only music or art. He should have preparation in the other subjects, too."

DECENTRALIZATION

Another change in schools involves management and decision-making. Decentralization—also called shared decision-making and school-based management—shifts control from the district level to groups of schools or to a single school, where administrators, teachers, parents, and community leaders evaluate the needs of students and plan an education system to meet them. Decision-makers at individual schools may determine textbooks, courses, activities, and budgets. In some cases, they decide what teachers or other employees will be hired.

In New York City, where decentralization began in the 1960s, some problems have occurred. Political ties and friendships became factors in getting certain jobs. Some local school boards were accused of mismanagement, extortion, or misappropriation of funds.

New York City Schools Chancellor Joseph A. Fernandez took office in 1990, with plans to introduce school-based management. As the superintendent of the Miami–Dade County schools in Florida, he had led such a plan that is considered one of the best in the nation. There, participating schools control their own personnel, curricula, and budgets. A committee composed of teachers, administrators, and parents deals with the issues that arise at each school.

Chicago also has a decentralized plan, but its design is different from New York's. The New York system has district school boards. In Chicago an elected team of parents, neighborhood residents, and teachers operates each school. The Chicago system also eliminated tenure for principals—they will not be able to keep their jobs solely because they have worked in the system for a given number of years. Michael Kirst, professor of education at Stanford University, calls this plan "precedent-breaking... the biggest change in American school control since the [early] 1900s."

The challenges for the Chicago schools are great. Seventy percent of the students live in families with incomes below the poverty line. Many parents did not finish high school. But parental interest has been strong. Parents attended meetings to discuss the new plan, and more than enough people ran for the demanding (but unpaid) school council jobs.

Salim Al-Nurridin, a community organizer on the South Side of Chicago, said, "This is about restructuring our community from the ground up." And Dan Solis, director of the United Neighborhood Organization, a Hispanic group, called the process "the largest experiment in grass-roots democracy the country has ever seen."

Early in 1990 some Chicago schools experienced problems. The parent-led councils dismissed principals at several schools. Critics charged that a few predominantly Hispanic councils had dismissed principals solely because they were white. Students protested by leaving classes, and parents complained at board of education meetings. Other problems have arisen because of language barriers, in cases where a principal does not speak Spanish and the council members know little English.

In spite of these problems, many people think that decentralization can be successful if certain guidelines are followed. Ann

Lynch, national PTA president, says that parents should first ask who wants decentralization and why: "Everyone involved in the school should examine the group proposing the change and decide whether their goals will fulfill everyone's needs."

YEAR-ROUND SCHOOLS

It is mid-July, and Jeff, age fifteen, is sitting in math class. Jeff lives in Los Angeles, where overcrowded buildings have led to a year-round schedule for the city's six hundred public schools. In the traditional schedule, summer was always vacation time. Now at least sixteen states, including Missouri, Texas, Nevada, Colorado, and Utah, operate some of their schools throughout the year. In most cases, students still attend school for the same number of days, with vacations distributed throughout the year.

In California, urban schools with large numbers of immigrants are especially crowded. In January 1990 a Los Angeles school official said, "We're simply running out of space. We need 42,000 elementary seats in the next two years. We can't find land fast enough, and we can't build schools fast enough." Operating the schools all year, with students attending school the same number of days as before, increases their capacity by about 33 percent. Year-round operation costs more money, but some costs are saved—for example, when students don't have to be transported to schools located far from their homes.

Many educators think the school year itself should be longer. Charles Ballinger, director of the National Association for Year-Round Education, calls the customary summer vacation "a disruption of the learning process." Supporters of year-round school attendance say that if U.S. students spent more days in school, achievement levels would rise. They point out that in Japan and Western Europe, students attend school about two months longer each year, sometimes for more hours per day.

But parents have complained that family activities and children's sports programs are interrupted by year-round schedules.

Child care can be a problem if vacations take place during months when summer camps are not open. And summer heat can make learning difficult in buildings that are not air-conditioned. A Los Angeles student who has experienced year-round school says, "It was a big adjustment. Some of my friends have a different schedule. But I've been able to get a better job during my vacations, because there is less competition."

HOME-BASE GUIDANCE

While some schools are staying open year round, others are redesigning programs. Rochester, New York, has implemented a "home-base guidance" system designed to give students more individual attention and to strengthen the family's ability to help children succeed in school.

Rochester's teachers play a central role in the plan. Teachers are counselors, or "case-managers," to about twenty students who can discuss courses, family, homework, or other concerns. Students meet with their teacher-counselors before class and at the end of the school day. Teachers also visit parents at home to discuss the student's progress or let them know about problems. By understanding students' needs, teachers can counsel them and connect them with social services or tutoring.

These reforms mean increased teacher responsibilities. Some teachers express concern that they are not trained in counseling. Some have also complained that they are functioning more as social workers than as teachers. Other teachers think home visits are useful. "It shows the students that you care about them," said one teacher. "Many parents are uncomfortable in the school setting, having had negative or intimidating experiences there during their own childhoods." Along with more work, the teachers received pay raises and are now the best-paid teachers outside of Alaska.

School-based management has also been implemented. Teachers, parents, and administrators are elected to make decisions about organization and methods used in the schools. It is hoped that these reforms will reduce some of Rochester's problems, including a high dropout rate (nearly one-third of all high school freshmen drop out before graduating); high rates of absenteeism; test scores below grade level; and an annual pregnancy rate of about 12 percent among girls ages fifteen to nineteen. Because these problems exist in many school systems, journalist Lisa W. Foderaro writes, "Rochester's program is being watched closely both because it is viewed as the most comprehensive and because this city of 241,000 is considered ethnically and socioeconomically average."

Interviewed by ABC News, Suzanne Johnston, principal of Wilson High School in Rochester, said, "When you walk into this building you are not just a number. Home-base makes sure that every youngster is recognized, nurtured, their families known. It's a real family-building situation."

Working with parents and developing mutual respect is also stressed at Central Park East, an effective secondary-school program in New York City that serves many lower-income students. The program was featured in "Crisis: Urban Education," a series for public television. Students at the school described the many benefits of their education; ability to think for themselves, self-confidence, learning healthful ways to deal with stress, and communication skills. As one poised young woman put it, "I am *not* a statistic."

AVOIDING NEGATIVE LABELS

Building self-confidence, a key component of successful programs like Central Park East, is stressed by educators. Studies show that although children typically begin their schooling eager to learn, many lose interest through the years. And one reason for this loss of enthusiasm is that some children are labeled as slow or less able to learn. This can cause a lack of self-confidence and become an obstacle to academic success.

David Elkind, professor of child study at Tufts University, says, "The worst thing we're doing with young children today in the public school system is labeling them at an early age." Dr. Elkind says that labeling is done at increasingly younger ages, leading to mislabeling. The risk is that a child will behave according to the low expectations communicated by other people.

In some U.S. schools, students are labeled as fast, average, or slow learners, then grouped with others who are similarly labeled in so-called tracks. They may take courses that are designated as fast, average, or slow track. Students may remain in the same track throughout high school.

Schools That Work, a U.S. Department of Education publication, discusses the importance of challenging *all* students and setting high expectations for performance: "Research indicates that schools often limit the opportunities of [disadvantaged] students. They are exposed to far less coursework than other students, and within the subjects they do take, they are not taught the reasoning skills needed to progress." The department recommends the reduction of rigid tracking which can "arbitrarily restrict student learning opportunities."

In some schools, students stay with the same group for every course. According to Karen Stone, a journalist with ABC News, "Kids on the fast track often get the best teachers and a challenging curriculum designed to stimulate critical thinking and problem solving." Jeannie Oakes, author and social scientist, says, "They write [lower-track students] off by giving them less and expecting less from them, and letting them choose to be less then they're really able to be."

Robert Slavin of Johns Hopkins University studied research about tracking versus mixed-ability (heterogeneous) grouping and concluded that tracking does not affect the achievement of either high- or low-ranked students. He concluded that tracking does not benefit "average" students either. Furthermore, people are concerned that a disproportionate number of minority students are found in lower track courses.

Many schools have reduced or eliminated tracking. At James Madison High School in Brooklyn, New York, tracking has been abolished in several subjects. Students of different ability levels attend the same classes and study the same subject matter. An English teacher says that "every kid at every level brings a different dimension to the material. And once you bring in a different dimension that maybe you never heard of before, you automatically start to think."

But many educators think that dividing students into groups according to ability is valid, at least for some subjects, such as math and science. They point out that students with widely different skills do not benefit equally when the same material is presented to everyone at once. Like many others, a Florida teacher claims that students with more academic talent deserve to maximize their opportunities, too.

Some schools have tried a system called cooperative learning, in which students study together in groups with others of different abilities. Students who learn more slowly may enjoy learning from fellow students. Students who learn more quickly help to explain the material to others. Figuring out how to teach a fellow student may enhance the faster student's understanding of the material. Frequently, cooperative learning includes a change in teaching methods—more discussion and "hands-on" learning and less lecturing, as teachers move around the room.

"It's to everyone's advantage," says Kevin Ryan, director of the Center for the Advancement of Ethics and Character at Boston University. "It's better for the average students because learning is active, not passive. The bright students can demonstrate their skill and not be bored while the teacher explains something five times. The slower students get the attention, help, and acceptance of their peers."

Some educators disagree. Linda K. Silverman, director of the Gifted Child Development Center in Denver, says, "Children come to school to learn something new. They are not supposed to be assisting the teacher or repeating material they knew four years ago or getting the grade for the cooperative learning group."

Along with the debate over tracking and ability groups, educators are reevaluating the concepts of bright, average, and slow. Dr. Henry M. Levin, of Stanford University, uses a fast-paced curriculum to help students labeled "slow learners." Dr. Levin's Accelerated Schools Project began in 1986 and has been used in some elementary schools to replace remedial instruction, which often relies upon drills and slower-paced reading materials. Educators worry that taking children out of class for remedial sessions can result in feelings of inferiority. "These kids are stigmatized and humiliated," claims Dr. Levin.

In Levin's program, students work with teacher aides in their own classrooms on faster-paced material that contains complex words and ideas. They discuss the material and write essays and stories. Students of different ability levels may work together in small learning teams. Teachers who have used the method say that it communicates positive expectations to students and leads to higher achievement. More individualized instruction also appears to be a key factor in the success of Levin's methods.

With so many programs for gifted students and for those with special needs, what happens to the so-called average kids—those in the middle? Sometimes these students, who make up the majority of the school population, feel ignored. In Trumbull, Connecticut, Project Academic was started in 1989 to give more attention to such students. Jacqueline Norcel, principal at Tashua Elementary School, where the program began, says, "The idea is that you don't have to be gifted to accomplish your goals and objectives. You have to have twelve characteristics. Those are: Be here; be on time; be a risk-taker (as in raising your hand); be prepared; be a goal-setter; be a listener; be polite; be responsible; be confident; be a tough worker; be a doer; be friendly."

Joan Goldberg, a teacher at Public School 6 in New York City, says, "There isn't a child in the world who doesn't have something that makes him stand out. It is the essence of our job not to let someone be just average. We have to find out what's inside kids and make them feel confident enough to show it off."

IMPROVING SCHOOLS THAT SERVE MINORITY STUDENTS

Many reform efforts aim to help minority students—African Americans, Native Americans, Mexican Americans, and Puerto Ricans—those "traditionally underserved" by the nation's education system, according to Shirley M. McBay, director of a recent study for the Quality Education for Minorities Project at the Massachusetts Institute of Technology.

The report said that schools should view "student achievement as the main criterion against which teachers, principals, and administrators are judged and rewarded." Toward that goal, the report recommends nutrition programs, multicultural curricula, smaller classes, and more aid for children living below the poverty line. It suggests that students take part in community service programs and that high school–age students spend the summer on college campuses increasing academic skills. The report also stressed the fact that, given the same advantages and opportunities, minority students' abilities are no different from those of others.

A highly regarded program was developed by Dr. James P. Comer, professor of child psychiatry at Yale University Medical School. Growing up in East Chicago, Indiana, in a poor family that lacked formal education, Dr. Comer learned firsthand how parental involvement can lead to academic success. His own parents supported their children's efforts in school and took them to museums and educational events. Dr. Comer and his four brothers and sisters have earned thirteen college degrees.

Dr. Comer has said, "I began to think about how you could make a difference for low-income kids, and I decided that the only place you could in our society—because you can't get to

Dr. James P. Comer believes that strong families and parental involvement in the schools help children succeed academically.

families earlier—is the school." His model includes a "school governance team"—parents, teachers, the principal, and other school staff who plan the operation of the school. Mental health teams in the schools help with special problems.

Comer's methods focus upon preventing rather than fixing problems. They aim to create a more personal environment in schools, characterized by mutual goals and respect. Dr. Wendy Winters, who has worked with Dr. Comer, says, "He knows people thrive in supportive environments. He believes they 'can do' and he wants to pass that on to teachers and parents."

In 1968 two New Haven elementary schools that had low academic performance records began using Comer's methods. As of 1984, the two schools ranked third and fourth in New Haven (ahead of several middle-income schools) on the Iowa Tests of Basic Skills. The number of behavior problems was greatly reduced, while student attendance was high—first and second among all of the city's schools. Teacher turnover also decreased.

The Comer model has improved student achievement in other schools and has been built into the curricula of teacher-training programs at several universities. In early 1990 plans were made to use the system in Washington, D.C., schools. The program has also received a $15 million grant from the Rockefeller Foundation.

Dr. Comer's goals of developing the "whole child"—socially, psychologically, and academically—embody sound principles of teaching, learning, and community involvement in the schools. These ideas can improve education for students from any background.

TEACHING STUDENTS TO THINK

A crucial part of improving education for all U.S. students is to help them gain skill in critical thinking—the ability to analyze information and use if effectively. For example, students should learn to solve problems with multiple steps and be able to gather and organize information for oral or written work, with sound arguments to back up their opinions. The ability to process new information and learn new methods of doing things is an essential tool for the future. How else will Americans cope with an increasingly technological workplace and with life in communities that include a wide range of people and ideas?

Earlier chapters discussed programs and teaching methods that promote critical thinking skills. Discussion, experimentation, and problem-solving are among the ways in which schools help students learn to think. As students ask questions and are required to back up their ideas, they become better thinkers.

Dr. Robert Marzano, a thinking-skills specialist, told ABC News that these approaches also keep students interested: "It's not very exciting to be put in an environment for six hours a day, 180 days a year, where your basic task is to take in information and give it back, and very close to the way you were given it."

Clearly schools have a great deal to consider as they implement reforms and try to prepare students for the twenty-first century. American schools are changing at many levels and in many different ways. Information about new teaching methods and school reforms is increasingly available, and educators say that schools and communities are more willing to try new techniques. Identifying the best educational structures, tools, and methods, and using them effectively in more schools, are major challenges for the 1990s.

CHAPTER ELEVEN

COMMUNITY INVOLVEMENT

"**WE** are all in this together," reads a sign at a Brooklyn, New York, high school. The spirit embodied in that sign may hold the key to reaching America's education goals for the twenty-first century. In 1988, Lloyd H. Elliot, president of George Washington University, called for such unified action:

> America's educational system must be significantly strengthened—from the earliest years of organized learning to the most advanced graduate years of study—and we can't walk away from this responsibility by simply passing legislation or even writing a check. The impetus has to come from a greater appreciation of learning on the part of parents, families, neighborhoods, and communities, as well as teachers and other professional school people. And it has to come from a working partnership among these individuals.

Increasingly, schools are looking for these "working partnerships"—resources and help from people and organizations in the community. These resources include financial and material help, as well as human capital. Partnerships with businesses have enabled schools to link education with careers and to motivate students by promising them a good job or higher education after graduation. Schools are also seeking stronger connections with families.

MORE FAMILY INVOLVEMENT

How did your parents influence your education, and how will you influence the education of your children? A sixteen-year-old says, "Our parents help, but we could use more. Both my parents work. I wish they could help me more on weekdays." A fourteen-year-old comments, "I know my mom will go to the school if I need help. She's always telling me, 'Get good grades! Don't mess around.'"

Parenting can have a strong effect upon school achievement. Says Pat Henry, first vice president of the national PTA, "Research has shown again and again that parents are children's first and most important teachers. Just having parents involved in their children's education helps children learn and having them involved in their children's schools improves those schools."

In order to involve more people in education, the National PTA is working to recruit more black and Hispanic parents into local chapters. It has translated its literature from English into other languages, and urges that PTA meetings be held at times when working parents can attend.

Educators believe it is imperative to reach out to families that need extra help to prepare their children for school. "It will be a more diversified group coming into our school system," says Dr. Samuel G. Sava, director of the National Association of Elementary School Principals. "Some children will be able to understand twelve thousand words and some only about four thousand words." Poor families, especially those without English proficiency, may "send children to school lacking the basic vocabulary needed in the first grade," says Sava. He points out that in homes where people spend most of their time and energy trying to meet basic survival needs, there is less time for conversation, doing homework together, or enjoying leisure activities as a family.

Parent involvement has been a key element in many school reforms. Dr. James Comer, whose widely praised New Haven, Connecticut, program emphasizes family-school involvement, says, "Parents have to believe in the school and the school staff has to believe in the parents. Working together is a way to break down the distrust and suspicion, to show they all have the children's interest at heart."

STUDENT EFFORTS

Many young people are also working to improve school and community life. In Sylvester, Georgia, teenagers formed a Youth Leadership Committee. Teens meet with a teacher adviser at the local office of the Save the Children Federation, a nonprofit organization that sponsors programs around the world, emphasizing community self-help. The Youth Leadership Committee has conducted surveys of the problems in its economically depressed area and has examined potential resources. Members also tutor younger children.

Other schools have programs in which students tutor fellow students. Some schools pair student tutors with younger children or those enrolled in special-education classes. "I watch out for her," a thirteen-year-old said of the third-grade girl whom he tutors. "She's smart, and she's fun to be with. I like being a teacher for someone else."

Journalist Katrine Ames interviewed teenage volunteers and concluded that, for many, "the sentiment 'I'm okay, who cares about you?' no longer prevails." In Detroit, seventeen-year-old George Smith spends afternoons tutoring younger kids and coaching them in sports. Other teens raise money for needy schools or families in their areas. A California student involved in an ecology project says, "It will be our gift to the younger generation." Arizona student Lizz Cohen points out, "If you're not involved, you'll never make a change. You can talk about it, but it's just talk."

INDIVIDUALS MAKE A DIFFERENCE

In 1981 a millionaire businessman named Eugene Lang visited the neighborhood in New York City where he had grown up to speak to the sixty-one graduating sixth-graders of Public School 121. He made an unusual promise: If the students would finish high school, he would pay for their college educations.

This was the start of Lang's "I Have a Dream" Foundation (IHAD), which distributes money donated by corporations and individuals and provides students with patrons who help them to cope with the problems of growing up and finishing school in difficult circumstances. "You have to keep reinvigorating them, rekindling their ambition, helping them overcome immediate problems—which may be emotional, economic, sociological— and get them back on track," says Lang.

Thirty-four people (more than 50 percent) in the 1981 group sponsored by the IHAD Foundation went on to college, part-time or full-time, a remarkable number in a group where more than half of the students usually drop out of high school.

Sponsors in more than thirty-one U.S. cities have emulated the "I Have a Dream" concept. Thousands of students are benefiting from their efforts. In Los Angeles a junior high "Dreamer" says, "I'm trying. People have encouraged me, and now I really know that I can get a chance to go." His mother says, "We have great hopes, great hopes."

COLLEGES BOLSTER PUBLIC SCHOOLS

Colleges have much to gain by helping to improve public education. Better schools mean more qualified applicants for the nation's colleges and broader support for education at every level. Some colleges have adopt-a-school plans; others provide tutoring programs that match high school students with faculty members or college students. Colleges may offer classes or summer sessions so that high school students can gain academic skills and learn about higher education.

Other collaborations help teachers to increase their knowledge and skills, ultimately benefiting students. Dr. Joseph C. Burke, provost of the State University of New York, says that using knowledge about teaching and learning to benefit children in the early grades is "the best use of our resources."

Several programs help students enter a chosen career. Only 10.1 percent of the nation's medical students are black, Hispanic, or Native American. In response to this problem, about one-third of the nation's 126 medical schools help minority and disadvantaged students who want to pursue medical careers.

One such program, at Albert Einstein College of Medicine in New York City, is funded by the state department of education and the Robert Wood Johnson Foundation. Poor and minority students attend the program. Participants take science courses where they gain laboratory experience and learn effective study habits. Older minority students serve as tutors. "I'll be the first in my family to go to college," says one eighteen-year-old. "My mom can hardly believe it." Program coordinator Louis Shing says that the program tries to show students that they *can* reach their goal and become doctors.

HELP FROM THE BUSINESS COMMUNITY

"The makings of a national disaster." That was the conclusion of David T. Kearns, former chairman of the Xerox Corporation, in regard to America's unqualified work force. "We cannot compete in a world-class economy without a world-class work force. And we cannot have a world-class work force without world-class schools." At an education conference sponsored by *Fortune* magazine, Kearns urged his fellow business leaders to improve education through direct involvement with the nation's schools.

Employers complain about clerical workers who do not read or spell correctly and about sales people who cannot do basic arithmetic. They criticize managers who cannot write clear memos and factory workers who cannot understand safety instructions. Much material in the workplace is written for those with twelfth-grade reading skills, yet about 60 million people read at the eighth-grade level or lower. One manufacturing executive said, "Workers need to be able to communicate better and understand directions. They need reading skills and logic."

To cope with these problems, "internal education" in reading, writing, listening, and mathematics has become common. About three-fourths of America's largest companies provide remedial education.

In order to strengthen the education system, many businesses are giving money directly to schools. The schools may use this money to improve buildings, buy more equipment, give extra training to staff members, or hire more teachers. Sometimes local school districts choose to develop magnet schools, specializing in science and mathematics, for example.

In 1989 the Pepsi-Cola Company announced its "Pepsi School Challenge," a plan to reduce dropout rates in inner-city schools. By maintaining a C average, meeting attendance requirements, and avoiding illegal drugs, students in Dallas and other cities will be eligible for college tuition credits.

In 1989, RJR Nabisco Inc. announced its "Next Century Schools" program—a plan to give $30 million to U.S. schools. Schools may apply for grants in order to try out innovative learning programs. Says RJR Nabisco chairman Louis V. Gerstner, Jr., "We're giving individuals on the front lines of education—teachers, principals, parents, and community-based coalitions—a chance to put their ideas into practice."

Eighth-grade art students work on a bulletin board, part of the Next Century Schools program sponsored by RJR Nabisco at Nathan Hale Intermediate School in Brooklyn, New York.

The General Electric Company has committed $20 million to troubled high schools, hoping to encourage more students to pursue higher education. The company has given money to the Manhattan Center for Science and Mathematics in New York City, as well as to schools in Kentucky, Wisconsin, Ohio, and North Carolina.

Citibank Corporation is also part of the effort to ensure that poor and inner-city youth are ready for college or a job after high school. It has pledged $20 million to urban schools in order to fund programs developed by educator Theodore Sizer, chairman of the department of education at Brown University. Sizer believes that, in order to give students adequate attention, each high school teacher should be assigned to no more than eighty students. In many urban schools teachers are responsible for twice this number of students.

Sizer thinks that schools should teach a few subjects thoroughly, rather than teaching many subjects superficially. Discussion, writing, and hands-on learning are major elements in his programs. The processes of research, writing, and debating that are used to learn one subject well are then used for later learning. Sizer questions the frequent use of standardized tests to measure achievement and suggests that some tests be eliminated. Instead students could prove their ability to carry out projects, assembling portfolios that display their accomplishments.

A number of U.S. schools—urban and rural, poor and affluent—have tried Sizer's method, which he describes as a set of ideas that can be adapted to different school settings. Sizer asserts, "There are no children for whom the habits of serious thought should be denied."

In addition to funding specific programs such as Sizer's, businesses may form partnerships with schools, as in "Adopt-a-School" programs. Employees become mentors or tutors for students. The company works to enhance and extend school programs. The National Association of School and Business Partnership Directors says that there has been a national increase in such partnerships, with about 150,000 of them around the United States.

Businesses may pay for student field trips or help students find summer jobs. In Stamford, Connecticut, the General Electric Company offers rewards for good attendance and bought backpacks and school supplies for every child in the elementary school that it sponsors. Mentors often follow a student's progress through school and beyond.

Describing the help he receives from his mentor, a twelfth-grader said, "He has given me such self-confidence. Now I feel like I can do whatever I set out to do." A junior at the same school said, "The tutoring after school made a big change in my grades. I get As and Bs now because I know I'm going to college. The better I do, the better I want to do."

These examples show how students may become more motivated as they look forward to higher education or a job after high school. Albert Shanker, president of the American Federation of Teachers, thinks this motivation is crucial: "Most students see no connection between what they've done in high school and the job they get after graduation. . . . Employers don't ask about the course new graduates took or the grades they got; the fact that a kid has a diploma is enough. So many kids think school is a big waste of time—and they treat it that way."

Shanker approves of school/business partnerships, as well as strong vocational programs in the schools. Some industrialized countries use apprenticeship systems to connect school and career. In West Germany, 60 percent of high school students between ages sixteen and eighteen compete for blue- and white-collar jobs that pay regular salaries. At their jobs, they work and receive special training. They continue to attend school during the week, taking some job-related courses. Shanker thinks that the United States should offer similar programs, producing workers with "the skills and habits of mind necessary for entry-level positions." These programs need not be as narrow or work-specific as some vocational training in the past.

In 1970, Philadelphia began the High School Academies program, which links school with jobs. Fourteen of the city's twenty-one public high schools combine academic and voca-tional training in such fields as auto mechanics and business. About 1,750 of the city's students work for $5.75 per hour after school and during the summer. Local businesses have provided major funding for the program. The program is considered successful: 93 percent of its students finish school, compared to 70 percent in the rest of the school population.

STUDENTS AND COMMUNITY SERVICE

Whether students are heading for jobs or more schooling, one persistent goal of American education has been to promote good citizenship. But a 1989 survey by the civil liberties group People for the American Way shows that this goal is in jeopardy. Author Peter D. Hart says that today's youth are only getting "half of

America's story.... although they clearly appreciate the democratic freedoms that, in their view, make theirs the 'best country in the world to live in,' they fail to perceive a need to reciprocate by exercising the duties and responsibilities of good citizenship." The social studies teachers who were surveyed claimed that students seem self-absorbed and concerned about enjoyment and financial success, showing little interest in politics or community involvement.

Hart concludes that there is a need for concerted efforts—by parents, educators, and administrators—"to teach young people not only about their rights and opportunities but about their obligations as citizens as well."

In 1983 the Carnegie Foundation for the Advancement of Teaching voiced this concern and proposed that high school students complete 120 hours of community service. This is now "a very fast growing activity," says foundation spokesman Robert A. Hochstein. How do students feel about community service requirements? "When I started at the soup kitchen, it was the first time I really got to be in such close contact with needy people," says a seventeen-year-old from an affluent New York City suburb. "I was scared and uncomfortable, but the homeless have beautiful stories to tell and meaningful things to say. I look forward to it every time I go now."

Students around the United States work in various places, including hospices, literacy programs, day-care centers, and the Red Cross. Some choose environmental projects. One student worked outdoors fighting beach erosion along the local coast.

Members of Congress are considering national service programs. In the spring of 1990 the Senate Labor Committee examined a community service program that would involve people from elementary school through old age. Education vouchers for college tuition might be given to young people in return for service. Legislators think that a service ethic would not only benefit young people but also fill gaps in the areas of social need that are not being met—hunger, homelessness, lack of child care for working mothers, and illiteracy. Some advocates of national service think that all citizens should be required to contribute one or two years to such a program.

Joseph S. Murphy, former Peace Corps volunteer and later chancellor of the City University of New York, says, "Suddenly we're waking up to the fact that we invested very little in our human and social infrastructure and that we've got some terrible deficits there.... What I think [volunteer work] will do is build into the lives of people in their education from the very outset that to live in a society is to live for more than just yourself but for the welfare of others." As the twenty-first century approaches, there is more talk about such human resources and community involvement. Many people think that this increasing involvement is one of the most promising outgrowths of the school reform movement.

CHAPTER TWELVE

LOOKING

TOWARD

THE FUTURE

AMERICA'S public schools now serve about 42 million students, offering tuition-free elementary and secondary education to every citizen as they have done for many decades. Unlike schools in other countries, such as Japan, U.S. schools serve a truly diverse population—people of different nationalities, races, religions, and economic levels. Schools provide extra services, such as sports and physical education, meals, field trips, cultural events, and after-school activities. They prepare young people for jobs and additional education. In many cases, education has enabled new generations of Americans to become upwardly mobile, socially and economically.

The education system allows people to continue learning at different stages of life. People who did not finish high school can study later on, to qualify for an "equivalency" diploma. People of all ages are enrolled in U.S. colleges. It is possible to study part-time or full-time, day or evening, and to combine jobs with schooling. We can learn throughout our lives.

LEARNING THROUGHOUT LIFE

"We want people who know how to learn," say colleges and businesses. When we "learn how to learn," or develop skills that enable us to keep learning throughout our lives, we are well-equipped to succeed in higher education, or as employees, business owners, and citizens. One of the national education goals for the year 2000 is that every American will be capable of lifelong learning. Such learning is essential for personal growth and enrichment and for the future of the nation.

Rapid changes in society mean that it is no longer enough to memorize facts, attain a certain level of skill, and then quit learning. The skills that were useful in an industrial society are less marketable in today's information society, says the National Association of Secondary School Principals. It notes three major shifts that have occurred during the past century: from specific training to "generalizable skills," from education that focuses upon one's own nation or continent to global education, and from basic skills to basic plus higher-order skills.

What does this mean to schools? Keeping up with new information in science, world events, and other subjects requires new approaches to teaching, with less emphasis on details and facts and more emphasis on concepts and research skills. One teacher put it this way: "The time has long passed when we can teach children all they need to know. The body of knowledge is too vast. But we can promote the joy of the thought process."

At the center of this higher-order thinking are critical thinking and problem-solving skills. "Learning how to learn" means that one can observe and investigate, analyze and evaluate, then practice to gain real mastery. It means being able to find information and evaluate the sources of that information. It requires an ability to organize and use information and to communicate effectively.

High school graduation, a traditional American rite of passage, is a proud moment for students, parents, and teachers alike.

For students, learning how to find information is vital. A high school student demonstrates this as she uses a library computer to get information for a science paper. By typing four words on the keyboard and hitting some other buttons, she gets a printout listing articles related to her topic, with brief summaries of their content. "This really speeds things up. It's a lifesaver," says the student.

Skills are part of lifelong learning, but attitudes are also important. How do we develop an ongoing desire to learn, the basis for lifelong learning? The answer to this vital question will determine the kinds of school programs we design. Experts claim that, beginning in childhood, each of us needs enough support and success to give us confidence in our ability to keep learning.

Many people also say that learning throughout life should spring from a desire to reach our own potential, rather than to compete with others. Psychologist Eda LeShan urges that children be given a learning environment that is "so rich in possibilities, so warm and supportive, so rich in learning experiences, that each child will find himself involved in a personal struggle *with himself* to learn more."

SCHOOLS OF EXCELLENCE

There are "good" schools all over the country—schools where students and teachers enjoy working together and where achievement is high. Many of these schools incorporate the elements described in previous sections—high levels of parent involvement, more personalized attention, and principals who work with the staff and students to develop a setting conducive to learning.

Educators have tried to pinpoint the sources of a positive school climate or atmosphere.

Roland S. Barth, senior lecturer in education at Harvard University, describes his vision of a good school as a community of learners—"a place in which everyone is teaching and everyone is learning—simultaneously under the same roof. Everything that goes on in a good school contributes to this end."

Barth wants schools to show more respect for diversity—and to use differences as opportunities for learning. He envisions a place where people ask questions—about curriculum, use of space, grading, grouping practices, discipline policies. He also thinks that schools should help people learn to be leaders: "A school can work to insure that everyone becomes a school leader in some ways and at some times. A school can fulfill no higher purpose than to teach all its members that they can make what they believe in happen and to encourage them to contribute to and benefit from the leadership of others."

Some high schools offer courses in leadership training. "It was the best course I took in school, without a doubt," says a recent graduate who took such a course in Rochester, New York. "I learned to take responsibility for what I get out of school and out of life. It improved the way I got involved in every other class and in my outside activities."

FUNDING: AN ONGOING DEBATE

The debate over how much money is needed for "good schools" and for child and family services is expected to continue during the 1990s. Some people say that money is not the critical issue— many high-quality schools manage on budgets that are similar to or even lower than schools that are less effective. The answer to problems is not money but how it is spent, say these people.

Yet many experts stress the need for preschool education, nutrition programs, drug abuse prevention, and other social programs. Such services cost money. Extra funding is also needed to repair buildings, replace textbooks and equipment, buy computers, and hire more teachers.

Where will extra money come from? Because of the federal budget deficit, this is an especially controversial issue. A number of Americans have suggested lowering the U.S. defense budget to provide more funding for education. A *New York Times* editorial proposed that by eliminating plans to build new weapons that would be used in the case of a war in Europe, the federal government would save about $77 billion a year over the next five years. In 1985, social activist Jane Midgley had advocated cutting defense spending because of "threats that are corroding our society from within": hunger, unemployment, homelessness, illiteracy, infant mortality, and crime. But the 1991 war in the Persian Gulf has increased military spending.

Other people say that a tax increase is the way to raise more money for schools. Still others contend that schools can be improved without spending more money, but by cutting certain nonacademic courses and programs from school budgets.

There is no easy answer to the question of where to get more money for education and other social programs. Decisions will ultimately depend upon the values and priorities that the nation—and we as individuals—choose to adopt.

A MAJOR CHALLENGE FOR THE 1990S

Educator Theodore Sizer says that the nation will need both imagination and staying power in order to improve education during coming years. Significant improvement will require creative solutions, and many programs will take years to show results.

In *Workforce 2000* authors William Johnston and Arthur Packer say that improving workers' education and skills is one of the greatest challenges for America in the twenty-first century: "In previous centuries, the wealth of nations was thought to consist of gold in the national treasury and jewels in the emperor's crown. In more recent years, wealth has often been equated with factories, mines, and production machinery within a nation's borders. As the miraculous rebirth of Europe and Japan after World War II has proven, however, the foundation of national wealth is really people—the human capital represented by their knowledge, skills, organizations, and motivations. . . . If this bright future is to be realized, the educational standards that have been established in the nation's schools must be raised dramatically."

In working toward improved education, everyone has something to contribute. Each person can take responsibility for his or her *own* learning. Parents can become more involved with their children's education and the work of the schools. In most communities, volunteers are needed in schools, libraries, literacy classes, and programs for young people. As citizens we can also vote and give feedback to political leaders about what we think is important.

"I have wondered if anything I do can make a difference," says a recent high school graduate who attends a community college. "I spend an evening a week tutoring two students from the high school I graduated from. Helping them move forward in life might not change the whole world, but it helps."

During the 1980s debates about public education broadened in scope. America examined its schools—their structure, methods, and curricula—and, in many cases, found them lacking. The publication of *A Nation at Risk* and other reports about public education in America sounded an alarm that has led to ongoing efforts toward improvement.

As 1990 began, America had a list of national education goals for the first time in history. Education reforms were in place, and many had proven to be effective. But in numerous schools needed changes have come slowly or not at all.

Will the 1990s be a time of real progress? The challenges to America's education system are formidable, but many people think that the nation has the talent and flexibility to meet them. The reform effort will be led by a new secretary of eduation, former Tennessee Governor Lamar Alexander. The son of two schoolteachers, he was appointed in December 1990. Our best efforts are needed if future Americans are to receive one of the most valuable assets a society can offer to its people: a high-quality education.

SELECTED BIBLIOGRAPHY

American Broadcasting Company (ABC News). *Burning Questions: America's Kids—Why They Flunk.* New York: Journal Graphics, 1988.

Benjamin, Robert. *Making Schools Work: A Reporter's Journey Through Some of America's Most Remarkable Classrooms.* New York: Continuum Publishing Corporation, 1981.

Bennett, William J. *First Lessons: A Report on Elementary Education in America.* Washington, D.C.: U.S. Department of Education, 1986.

————. *Our Children and Our Country.* New York: Simon and Schuster, 1986.

Boyer, Ernest L. *High School: A Report on Secondary Education in America.* New York: Harper and Row, 1983.

Carnegie Forum on Education and the Economy: Task Force on Teaching as a Profession. *A Nation Prepared: Teachers for the 21st Century.* New York: Carnegie Corporation, 1986.

Comer, James P. *School Power: Implications of an Intervention Project.* New York: Free Press, 1980.

Committee for Economic Development. *Children in Need: Investment Strategies for the Educationally Disadvantaged.* New York, 1987.

Davidson, Jack L., and Margaret Montgomery. *An Analysis of Reports on the Status of Education in America: Findings, Recommendations, and Implications.* Tyler, Tex.: Tyler Independent School District, 1984.

Davis, Bertha, and Dorothy Arnof. *How to Fix What's Wrong with Our Schools.* New York: Ticknor and Fields, 1983.

Education Commission of the States. *A Summary of Major Reports on Education.* Denver, 1983.

Fantini, Mario D. *Public Schools of Choice.* New York: Simon and Schuster, 1973.

Featherstone, Joseph. *Schools Where Children Learn.* New York: Liveright, 1972.

Goodlad, John. *A Place Called School: Prospects for the Future.* Hightstown, N.J.; McGraw-Hill, 1983.

Gross, Ronald and Beatrice, eds. *The Great School Debate.* New York: Simon & Schuster, 1985.

——. *Radical School Reform.* New York: Simon and Schuster, 1969.

Hart, Peter D. *Democracy's Next Generation.* Washington, D.C.: People for the American Way, 1989.

Johnston, William B., and Arnold E. Packer. *Workforce 2000: Work and Workers for the 21st Century.* Indianapolis: Hudson Institute, 1987.

Kidder, Tracy. *Among Schoolchildren.* Boston: Houghton Mifflin Co., 1989.

Maeroff, Gene. *Don't Blame the Kids: The Problem with America's Public Schools.* New York: McGraw-Hill, 1982.

Midgley, Jane. *The Women's Budget.* Philadelphia: Women's International League for Peace and Freedom, 1985.

National Center for Education Statistics. *Digest for Education Statistics.* Washington, D.C.: U.S. Department of Education, 1989.

——. *Projections of Educational Statistics 1990-91.* Washington, D.C.: U.S. Department of Education, 1989.

National Commission on Excellence in Education. *A Nation at Risk: A Report to the Nation and the Secretary of Education.* Washington, D.C.: U.S. Department of Education, April 1983.

National Governors Association. *Time for Results: The Governors' Report on Education.* Washington, D.C.: 1986.

Oakes, Jeannie. *Keeping Track.* New Haven: Yale University Press, 1985.

Ravitch, Diane. *The Schools We Deserve: Reflections on the Educational Crises of Our Times.* New York: Basic Books, 1985.

————. *The Troubled Crusade: American Education 1945–1980.* New York: Basic Books, 1983.

Task Force on Education for Economic Growth. *Action for Excellence: A Comprehensive Plan to Improve Our Nation's Schools.* Denver, Colo.: Education Commission of the States, 1983.

U.S. Department of Education. *Dealing with Dropouts: The Urban Superintendents' Call to Action.* Washington, D.C.: U.S. Government Printing Office, 1987.

Zigler, Edward, and Jeanette Valentine. *Project Head Start: A Legacy of the War on Poverty.* New York: Free Press, 1979.

Zinsser, William K. *Writing to Learn.* New York: Harper and Row, 1988.

INDEX

ACKNOWLEDGMENTS

The publisher wishes to thank Judith Cohen, resource coordinator; Michael Mazun, administrative assistant; and the staff and students of Nathan Hale Intermediate School 293, Brooklyn, New York, for their assistance with photographs of their school.

Photo credits: AP/Wide World: 27, 109. The Bettmann Archive: 13. The Cincinnati Enquirer/Doug Cochran: 92. Comstock/© Russ Kinne: 37. Comstock/© Sven Martson: 125. Paul Conklin/Monkmeyer Press Photo Service: 86. © Bob Daemmrich; cover. © Shelley Gazin/The Image Works: 62. Michael Mazun/Nathan Hale Intermediate School: 43, 51, 53, 118. Reuters/Bettmann: 4. © Erika Stone 1987: 77. David S. Strickler/Monkmeyer Press Photo Service: 23.